FREE Study Skills DVD Offer

Dear Customer,

Thank you for your purchase from Mometrix! We consider it an honor and privilege that you have purchased our product and want to ensure your satisfaction.

As a way of showing our appreciation and to help us better serve you, we have developed a Study Skills DVD that we would like to give you for <u>FREE</u>. **This DVD covers our "best practices" for studying for your exam, from using our study materials to preparing for the day of the test.**

All that we ask is that you email us your feedback that would describe your experience so far with our product. Good, bad or indifferent, we want to know what you think!

To get your **FREE Study Skills DVD**, email <u>freedvd@mometrix.com</u> with "FREE STUDY SKILLS DVD" in the subject line and the following information in the body of the email:

  a. The name of the product you purchased.

  b. Your product rating on a scale of 1-5, with 5 being the highest rating.

  c. Your feedback. It can be long, short, or anything in-between, just your impressions and experience so far with our product. Good feedback might include how our study material met your needs and will highlight features of the product that you found helpful.

  d. Your full name and shipping address where you would like us to send your free DVD.

If you have any questions or concerns, please don't hesitate to contact me directly.

Thanks again!

Sincerely,

Jay Willis
Vice President
<u>jay.willis@mometrix.com</u>
1-800-673-8175

ACT Aspire

SUCCESS STRATEGIES
Grade 7

ACT Aspire Test Review for the
ACT Aspire Assessments

Dear Future Exam Success Story:

First of all, **THANK YOU** for purchasing Mometrix study materials!

Second, congratulations! You are one of the few determined test-takers who are committed to doing whatever it takes to excel on your exam. **You have come to the right place.** We developed these study materials with one goal in mind: to deliver you the information you need in a format that's concise and easy to use.

In addition to optimizing your guide for the content of the test, we've outlined our recommended steps for breaking down the preparation process into small, attainable goals so you can make sure you stay on track.

We've also analyzed the entire test-taking process, identifying the most common pitfalls and showing how you can overcome them and be ready for any curveball the test throws you.

Standardized testing is one of the biggest obstacles on your road to success, which only increases the importance of doing well in the high-pressure, high-stakes environment of test day. Your results on this test could have a significant impact on your future, and this guide provides the information and practical advice to help you achieve your full potential on test day.

Your success is our success

We would love to hear from you! If you would like to share the story of your exam success or if you have any questions or comments in regard to our products, please contact us at **800-673-8175** or **support@mometrix.com**.

Thanks again for your business and we wish you continued success!

Sincerely,
The Mometrix Test Preparation Team

Need more help? Check out our flashcards at: http://MometrixFlashcards.com/ACTAspire

TABLE OF CONTENTS

Introduction

Thank you for purchasing this resource! You have made the choice to prepare yourself for a test that could have a huge impact on your future, and this guide is designed to help you be fully ready for test day. Obviously, it's important to have a solid understanding of the test material, but you also need to be prepared for the unique environment and stressors of the test, so that you can perform to the best of your abilities.

For this purpose, the first section that appears in this guide is the **Success Strategies**. We've devoted countless hours to meticulously researching what works and what doesn't, and we've boiled down our findings to the five most impactful steps you can take to improve your performance on the test. We start at the beginning with study planning and move through the preparation process, all the way to the testing strategies that will help you get the most out of what you know when you're finally sitting in front of the test.

We recommend that you start preparing for your test as far in advance as possible. However, if you've bought this guide as a last-minute study resource and only have a few days before your test, we recommend that you skip over the first two Success Strategies since they address a long-term study plan.

If you struggle with **test anxiety**, we strongly encourage you to check out our recommendations for how you can overcome it. Test anxiety is a formidable foe, but it can be beaten, and we want to make sure you have the tools you need to defeat it.

Success Strategy #1 – Plan Big, Study Small

There's a lot riding on your performance. If you want to ace this test, you're going to need to keep your skills sharp and the material fresh in your mind. You need a plan that lets you review everything you need to know while still fitting in your schedule. We'll break this strategy down into three categories.

Information Organization

Start with the information you already have: the official test outline. From this, you can make a complete list of all the concepts you need to cover before the test. Organize these concepts into groups that can be studied together, and create a list of any related vocabulary you need to learn so you can brush up on any difficult terms. You'll want to keep this vocabulary list handy once you actually start studying since you may need to add to it along the way.

Time Management

Once you have your set of study concepts, decide how to spread them out over the time you have left before the test. Break your study plan into small, clear goals so you have a manageable task for each day and know exactly what you're doing. Then just focus on one small step at a time. When you manage your time this way, you don't need to spend hours at a time studying. Studying a small block of content for a short period each day helps you retain information better and avoid stressing over how much you have left to do. You can relax knowing that you have a plan to cover everything in time. In order for this strategy to be effective though, you have to start studying early and stick to your schedule. Avoid the exhaustion and futility that comes from last-minute cramming!

Study Environment

The environment you study in has a big impact on your learning. Studying in a coffee shop, while probably more enjoyable, is not likely to be as fruitful as studying in a quiet room. It's important to keep distractions to a minimum. You're only planning to study for a short block of time, so make the most of it. Don't pause to check your phone or get up to find a snack. It's also important to **avoid multitasking**. Research has consistently shown that multitasking will make your studying dramatically less effective. Your study area should also be comfortable and well-lit so you don't have the distraction of straining your eyes or sitting on an uncomfortable chair.

The time of day you study is also important. You want to be rested and alert. Don't wait until just before bedtime. Study when you'll be most likely to comprehend and remember. Even better, if you know what time of day your test will be, set that time aside for study. That way your brain will be used to working on that subject at that specific time and you'll have a better chance of recalling information.

Finally, it can be helpful to team up with others who are studying for the same test. Your actual studying should be done in as isolated an environment as possible, but the work of organizing the information and setting up the study plan can be divided up. In between study sessions, you can discuss with your teammates the concepts that you're all studying and quiz each other on the details. Just be sure that your teammates are as serious about the test as you are. If you find that your study time is being replaced with social time, you might need to find a new team.

Success Strategy #2 – Make Your Studying Count

You're devoting a lot of time and effort to preparing for this test, so you want to be absolutely certain it will pay off. This means doing more than just reading the content and hoping you can remember it on test day. It's important to make every minute of study count. There are two main areas you can focus on to make your studying count:

Retention

It doesn't matter how much time you study if you can't remember the material. You need to make sure you are retaining the concepts. To check your retention of the information you're learning, try recalling it at later times with minimal prompting. Try carrying around flashcards and glance at one or two from time to time or ask a friend who's also studying for the test to quiz you.

To enhance your retention, look for ways to put the information into practice so that you can apply it rather than simply recalling it. If you're using the information in practical ways, it will be much easier to remember. Similarly, it helps to solidify a concept in your mind if you're not only reading it to yourself but also explaining it to someone else. Ask a friend to let you teach them about a concept you're a little shaky on (or speak aloud to an imaginary audience if necessary). As you try to summarize, define, give examples, and answer your friend's questions, you'll understand the concepts better and they will stay with you longer. Finally, step back for a big picture view and ask yourself how each piece of information fits with the whole subject. When you link the different concepts together and see them working together as a whole, it's easier to remember the individual components.

Finally, practice showing your work on any multi-step problems, even if you're just studying. Writing out each step you take to solve a problem will help solidify the process in your mind, and you'll be more likely to remember it during the test.

Modality

Modality simply refers to the means or method by which you study. Choosing a study modality that fits your own individual learning style is crucial. No two people learn best in exactly the same way, so it's important to know your strengths and use them to your advantage.

For example, if you learn best by visualization, focus on visualizing a concept in your mind and draw an image or a diagram. Try color-coding your notes, illustrating them, or creating symbols that will trigger your mind to recall a learned concept. If you learn best by hearing or discussing information, find a study partner who learns the same way or read aloud to yourself. Think about how to put the information in your own words. Imagine that you are giving a lecture on the topic and record yourself so you can listen to it later.

For any learning style, flashcards can be helpful. Organize the information so you can take advantage of spare moments to review. Underline key words or phrases. Use different colors for different categories. Mnemonic devices (such as creating a short list in which every item starts with the same letter) can also help with retention. Find what works best for you and use it to store the information in your mind most effectively and easily.

Success Strategy #3 – Practice the Right Way

Your success on test day depends not only on how many hours you put into preparing, but also on whether you prepared the right way. It's good to check along the way to see if your studying is paying off. One of the most effective ways to do this is by taking practice tests to evaluate your progress. Practice tests are useful because they show exactly where you need to improve. Every time you take a practice test, pay special attention to these three groups of questions:

- The questions you got wrong
- The questions you had to guess on, even if you guessed right
- The questions you found difficult or slow to work through

This will show you exactly what your weak areas are, and where you need to devote more study time. Ask yourself why each of these questions gave you trouble. Was it because you didn't understand the material? Was it because you didn't remember the vocabulary? Do you need more repetitions on this type of question to build speed and confidence? Dig into those questions and figure out how you can strengthen your weak areas as you go back to review the material.

Additionally, many practice tests have a section explaining the answer choices. It can be tempting to read the explanation and think that you now have a good understanding of the concept. However, an explanation likely only covers part of the question's broader context. Even if the explanation makes sense, **go back and investigate** every concept related to the question until you're positive you have a thorough understanding.

As you go along, keep in mind that the practice test is just that: practice. Memorizing these questions and answers will not be very helpful on the actual test because it is unlikely to have any of the same exact questions. If you only know the right answers to the sample questions, you won't be prepared for the real thing. **Study the concepts** until you understand them fully, and then you'll be able to answer any question that shows up on the test.

It's important to wait on the practice tests until you're ready. If you take a test on your first day of study, you may be overwhelmed by the amount of material covered and how much you need to learn. Work up to it gradually.

On test day, you'll need to be prepared for answering questions, managing your time, and using the test-taking strategies you've learned. It's a lot to balance, like a mental marathon that will have a big impact on your future. Like training for a marathon, you'll need to start slowly and work your way up. When test day arrives, you'll be ready.

Start with what you've read in the first two Success Strategies—plan your course and study in the way that works best for you. If you have time, consider using multiple study resources to get different approaches to the same concepts. It can be helpful to see difficult concepts from more than one angle. Then find a good source for practice tests. Many times, the test website will suggest potential study resources or provide sample tests.

Practice Test Strategy

When you're ready to start taking practice tests, follow this strategy:

Untimed and Open-Book Practice

Take the first test with no time constraints and with your notes and study guide handy. Take your time and focus on applying the strategies you've learned.

Timed and Open-Book Practice

Take the second practice test open-book as well, but set a timer and practice pacing yourself to finish in time.

Timed and Closed-Book Practice

Take any other practice tests as if it were test day. Set a timer and put away your study materials. Sit at a table or desk in a quiet room, imagine yourself at the testing center, and answer questions as quickly and accurately as possible.

Keep repeating timed and closed-book tests on a regular basis until you run out of practice tests or it's time for the actual test. Your mind will be ready for the schedule and stress of test day, and you'll be able to focus on recalling the material you've learned.

Success Strategy #4 – Pace Yourself

Once you're fully prepared for the material on the test, your biggest challenge on test day will be managing your time. Just knowing that the clock is ticking can make you panic even if you have plenty of time left. Work on pacing yourself so you can build confidence against the time constraints of the exam. Pacing is a difficult skill to master, especially in a high-pressure environment, so **practice is vital**.

Set time expectations for your pace based on how much time is available. For example, if a section has 60 questions and the time limit is 30 minutes, you know you have to average 30 seconds or less per question in order to answer them all. Although 30 seconds is the hard limit, set 25 seconds per question as your goal, so you reserve extra time to spend on harder questions. When you budget extra time for the harder questions, you no longer have any reason to stress when those questions take longer to answer.

Don't let this time expectation distract you from working through the test at a calm, steady pace, but keep it in mind so you don't spend too much time on any one question. Recognize that taking extra time on one question you don't understand may keep you from answering two that you do understand later in the test. If your time limit for a question is up and you're still not sure of the answer, mark it and move on, and come back to it later if the time and the test format allow. If the testing format doesn't allow you to return to earlier questions, just make an educated guess; then put it out of your mind and move on.

On the easier questions, be careful not to rush. It may seem wise to hurry through them so you have more time for the challenging ones, but it's not worth missing one if you know the concept and just didn't take the time to read the question fully. Work efficiently but make sure you understand the question and have looked at all of the answer choices, since more than one may seem right at first.

Even if you're paying attention to the time, you may find yourself a little behind at some point. You should speed up to get back on track, but do so wisely. Don't panic; just take a few seconds less on each question until you're caught up. Don't guess without thinking, but do look through the answer choices and eliminate any you know are wrong. If you can get down to two choices, it is often worthwhile to guess from those. Once you've chosen an answer, move on and don't dwell on any that you skipped or had to hurry through. If a question was taking too long, chances are it was one of the harder ones, so you weren't as likely to get it right anyway.

On the other hand, if you find yourself getting ahead of schedule, it may be beneficial to slow down a little. The more quickly you work, the more likely you are to make a careless mistake that will affect your score. You've budgeted time for each question, so don't be afraid to spend that time. Practice an efficient but careful pace to get the most out of the time you have.

Test-Taking Strategies

This section contains a list of test-taking strategies that you may find helpful as you work through the test. By taking what you know and applying logical thought, you can maximize your chances of answering any question correctly!

It is very important to realize that every question is different and every person is different: no single strategy will work on every question, and no single strategy will work for every person. That's why we've included all of them here, so you can try them out and determine which ones work best for different types of questions and which ones work best for you.

Question Strategies

Read Carefully

Read the question and answer choices carefully. Don't miss the question because you misread the terms. You have plenty of time to read each question thoroughly and make sure you understand what is being asked. Yet a happy medium must be attained, so don't waste too much time. You must read carefully, but efficiently.

Contextual Clues

Look for contextual clues. If the question includes a word you are not familiar with, look at the immediate context for some indication of what the word might mean. Contextual clues can often give you all the information you need to decipher the meaning of an unfamiliar word. Even if you can't determine the meaning, you may be able to narrow down the possibilities enough to make a solid guess at the answer to the question.

Prefixes

If you're having trouble with a word in the question or answer choices, try dissecting it. Take advantage of every clue that the word might include. Prefixes and suffixes can be a huge help. Usually they allow you to determine a basic meaning. Pre- means before, post- means after, pro - is positive, de- is negative. From prefixes and suffixes, you can get an idea of the general meaning of the word and try to put it into context.

Hedge Words

Watch out for critical hedge words, such as *likely, may, can, sometimes, often, almost, mostly, usually, generally, rarely*, and *sometimes*. Question writers insert these hedge phrases to cover every possibility. Often an answer choice will be wrong simply because it leaves no room for exception. Be on guard for answer choices that have definitive words such as *exactly* and *always*.

Switchback Words

Stay alert for *switchbacks*. These are the words and phrases frequently used to alert you to shifts in thought. The most common switchback words are *but, although*, and *however*. Others include *nevertheless, on the other hand, even though, while, in spite of, despite, regardless of*. Switchback words are important to catch because they can change the direction of the question or an answer choice.

Face Value

When in doubt, use common sense. Accept the situation in the problem at face value. Don't read too much into it. These problems will not require you to make wild assumptions. If you have to go beyond creativity and warp time or space in order to have an answer choice fit the question, then you should move on and consider the other answer choices. These are normal problems rooted in reality. The applicable relationship or explanation may not be readily apparent, but it is there for you to figure out. Use your common sense to interpret anything that isn't clear.

Answer Choice Strategies

Answer Selection

The most thorough way to pick an answer choice is to identify and eliminate wrong answers until only one is left, then confirm it is the correct answer. Sometimes an answer choice may immediately seem right, but be careful. The test writers will usually put more than one reasonable answer choice on each question, so take a second to read all of them and make sure that the other choices are not equally obvious. As long as you have time left, it is better to read every answer choice than to pick the first one that looks right without checking the others.

Answer Choice Families

An answer choice family consists of two (in rare cases, three) answer choices that are very similar in construction and cannot all be true at the same time. If you see two answer choices that are direct opposites or parallels, one of them is usually the correct answer. For instance, if one answer choice says that quantity x increases and another either says that quantity x decreases (opposite) or says that quantity y increases (parallel), then those answer choices would fall into the same family. An answer choice that doesn't match the construction of the answer choice family is more likely to be incorrect. Most questions will not have answer choice families, but when they do appear, you should be prepared to recognize them.

Eliminate Answers

Eliminate answer choices as soon as you realize they are wrong, but make sure you consider all possibilities. If you are eliminating answer choices and realize that the last one you are left with is also wrong, don't panic. Start over and consider each choice again. There may be something you missed the first time that you will realize on the second pass.

Avoid Fact Traps

Don't be distracted by an answer choice that is factually true but doesn't answer the question. You are looking for the choice that answers the question. Stay focused on what the question is asking for so you don't accidentally pick an answer that is true but incorrect. Always go back to the question and make sure the answer choice you've selected actually answers the question and is not merely a true statement.

Extreme Statements

In general, you should avoid answers that put forth extreme actions as standard practice or proclaim controversial ideas as established fact. An answer choice that states the "process should be used in certain situations, if…" is much more likely to be correct than one that states the "process should be discontinued completely." The first is a calm rational statement and doesn't even make a

- 8 -

definitive, uncompromising stance, using a hedge word *if* to provide wiggle room, whereas the second choice is a radical idea and far more extreme.

Benchmark

As you read through the answer choices and you come across one that seems to answer the question well, mentally select that answer choice. This is not your final answer, but it's the one that will help you evaluate the other answer choices. The one that you selected is your benchmark or standard for judging each of the other answer choices. Every other answer choice must be compared to your benchmark. That choice is correct until proven otherwise by another answer choice beating it. If you find a better answer, then that one becomes your new benchmark. Once you've decided that no other choice answers the question as well as your benchmark, you have your final answer.

Predict the Answer

Before you even start looking at the answer choices, it is often best to try to predict the answer. When you come up with the answer on your own, it is easier to avoid distractions and traps because you will know exactly what to look for. The right answer choice is unlikely to be word-for-word what you came up with, but it should be a close match. Even if you are confident that you have the right answer, you should still take the time to read each option before moving on.

General Strategies

Tough Questions

If you are stumped on a problem or it appears too hard or too difficult, don't waste time. Move on! Remember though, if you can quickly check for obviously incorrect answer choices, your chances of guessing correctly are greatly improved. Before you completely give up, at least try to knock out a couple of possible answers. Eliminate what you can and then guess at the remaining answer choices before moving on.

Check Your Work

Since you will probably not know every term listed and the answer to every question, it is important that you get credit for the ones that you do know. Don't miss any questions through careless mistakes. If at all possible, try to take a second to look back over your answer selection and make sure you've selected the correct answer choice and haven't made a costly careless mistake (such as marking an answer choice that you didn't mean to mark). This quick double check should more than pay for itself in caught mistakes for the time it costs.

Pace Yourself

It's easy to be overwhelmed when you're looking at a page full of questions; your mind is confused and full of random thoughts, and the clock is ticking down faster than you would like. Calm down and maintain the pace that you have set for yourself. Especially as you get down to the last few minutes of the test, don't let the small numbers on the clock make you panic. As long as you are on track by monitoring your pace, you are guaranteed to have time for each question.

Don't Rush

It is very easy to make errors when you are in a hurry. Maintaining a fast pace in answering questions is pointless if it makes you miss questions that you would have gotten right otherwise. Test writers like to include distracting information and wrong answers that seem right. Taking a little extra time to avoid careless mistakes can make all the difference in your test score. Find a pace that allows you to be confident in the answers that you select.

Keep Moving

Panicking will not help you pass the test, so do your best to stay calm and keep moving. Taking deep breaths and going through the answer elimination steps you practiced can help to break through a stress barrier and keep your pace.

Final Notes

The combination of a solid foundation of content knowledge and the confidence that comes from practicing your plan for applying that knowledge is the key to maximizing your performance on test day. As your foundation of content knowledge is built up and strengthened, you'll find that the strategies included in this chapter become more and more effective in helping you quickly sift through the distractions and traps of the test to isolate the correct answer.

Now it's time to move on to the test content chapters of this book, but be sure to keep your goal in mind. As you read, think about how you will be able to apply this information on the test. If you've already seen sample questions for the test and you have an idea of the question format and style, try to come up with questions of your own that you can answer based on what you're reading. This will give you valuable practice applying your knowledge in the same ways you can expect to on test day.

Good luck and good studying!

Mathematics

Ratio and proportion

A ratio is a comparison of two numbers by division. The ratio of a to b, where $b \neq 0$, can be written as

a to b

$a:b$

$\dfrac{a}{b}$

A proportion is a statement of equality between two ratios. For example, $\dfrac{a}{b} = \dfrac{c}{d}$, where $b \neq 0$ and $d \neq 0$, is a proportion equating the ratios $\dfrac{a}{b}$ and $\dfrac{c}{d}$.

Integer

The set of integers includes whole numbers and their opposites: $\{...,-3,-2,-1,0,1,2,3...\}$.

Rational number

A rational number is a real number which can be written as a ratio of two integers a and b, where $b \neq 0$ so long as the second is not zero; in other words, any rational number can be expressed in fractional form $\dfrac{a}{b}$, where $b \neq 0$. Rational numbers include whole numbers, fractions, terminating, and repeating decimals.

Example

Write each rational number as a fraction

- 3
- 0.6

Since dividing any number by one does not change its value, a whole number can be written as a fraction with a denominator of 1. So, $3 = \dfrac{3}{1}$.

The six in 0.6 is in the tenths place. The number six-tenths can also be written as $\dfrac{6}{10}$, which reduces to $\dfrac{3}{5}$.

<u>Example</u>

    Simply each expression

$$\frac{2}{3} + \frac{1}{2}$$

$$\frac{2}{3} - \frac{1}{2}$$

When combining fractions, it is helpful to write them so that they have the same denominator.

1.

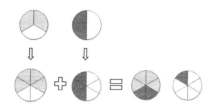

$$\frac{2}{3} = \frac{4}{6} \qquad \frac{1}{2} = \frac{3}{6}$$
$$\frac{4}{6} + \frac{3}{6} = \frac{7}{6} = 1\frac{1}{6}$$

2.

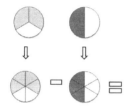

$$\frac{4}{6} - \frac{3}{6} = \frac{1}{6}$$

<u>Example</u>

    Simplify each expression

$$\frac{1}{2} \times \frac{2}{3}$$

$$\frac{1}{8} \div \frac{1}{2}$$

The numerator of the product of two fractions is the product of their numerators; $1 \times 2 = 2$. Likewise, the denominator of the product of two fractions is the product of their denominators: $2 \times 3 = 6$. Reduce the resulting fraction if necessary.

$$\frac{1}{2} \times \frac{2}{3} = \frac{2}{6} = \frac{1}{3}$$

When dividing fractions, rewrite the expression as the product of the first fraction and the reciprocal (or multiplicative inverse) of the second. Reduce if necessary.

$$\frac{1}{8} \div \frac{1}{2} = \frac{1}{8} \times \frac{2}{1} = \frac{2}{8} = \frac{1}{4};$$

- 13 -

<u>Example</u>

Convert each fraction to a decimal.

$$\frac{4}{5}$$

$$\frac{5}{6}$$

A fraction is a quotient of two numbers such that the denominator is not zero. So, one way to convert a fraction to a decimal is to divide the denominator into the numerator. The resulting decimal will either terminate or repeat.

$$\frac{4}{5} = 4 \div 5 = 0.8$$

```
      0.8
  5 | 4.0
      0  ↓
      4  0
      4  0
         0
```

$$\frac{5}{6} = 5 \div 6 = 0.8\overline{3}$$

```
      0.833...
  6 | 5.000...
      0  ↓
      5  0
      4  8 ↓
         20
         18 ↓
         20
         18
          2
```

Percentage

One *Percent* means one part per hundred, so a percentage is the ratio of a number to 100. For example, 42% can be written as the ratio $\frac{42}{100}$ or its reduced equivalent, $\frac{21}{50}$.

<u>Example</u>

Write each percentage as a simplified fraction and as a decimal

- 32%
- 135%

A percentage is a ratio of a number to 100.

$$32\% = \frac{32}{100} = \frac{8}{25} \ or \ \frac{32}{100} = 0.32$$

- 14 -

$$135\% = \frac{135}{100} = 1\frac{35}{100} = 1\frac{7}{20}$$

$$\frac{135}{100} = 1\frac{35}{100} = 1.35$$

Example

Write each number as a percentage

$$\frac{4}{5}$$

$$\frac{2}{3}$$

$$0.23 = \frac{23}{100} = 23\%$$

$$\frac{4}{5} = \frac{80}{100} = 80\%$$

$$\frac{2}{3} = 0.\overline{6} = 66.\overline{6}\%$$

Example

Express the shaded portion of the circle as a fraction, a decimal, and a percentage.

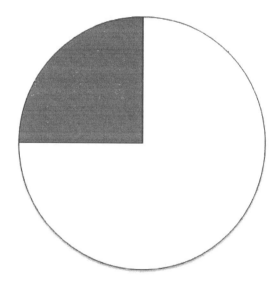

¼ of the circle's area is shaded. $\frac{1}{4} = 0.25 = \frac{25}{100} = 25\%$.

Determining whether or not two ratios form a proportion

Two ratios form a proportion if they are equal. One way to determine if two ratios are equal is to write each ratio as a fraction (as long as neither contains a zero in its denominator) and then cross-multiply: that is, multiply the numerator of the first fraction and the denominator of the second;

- 15 -

then, multiply the denominator of the first fraction and the numerator of the second. If these two products are equal, the ratios are equal and therefore form a proportion. $\frac{a}{b} = \frac{c}{d}$ if and only if $a \times d = b \times c$. For example, $\frac{2}{3} = \frac{12}{18}$, and $2 \times 18 = 3 \times 12 = 36$.

Unit rate

A unit rate is a ratio of two different types of numbers, the second of which is always one. For example, a unit rate can be the number of miles driven in one hour (miles per hour), the price for one ounce of cereal (cents per ounce), or an hourly wage (dollars per hour).

<u>Example</u>

A girl walks half a mile in fifteen minutes. Calculate the unit rate in miles per hour

Since there are sixty minutes in an hour, fifteen minutes is a quarter of an hour: $\frac{15}{60} = \frac{1}{4}$. Since the girl walks ½ mile in ¼ hour, her rate can be written as $\frac{\frac{1}{2}\text{ mile}}{\frac{1}{4}\text{ hour}}$. To determine the unit rate, simplify the fraction so that the denominator is one hour. One way to divide by the fraction $\frac{1}{4}$ is to instead multiply by its reciprocal $\frac{4}{1}$. We get $\frac{1}{2} \div \frac{1}{4} = \frac{1}{2} \times \frac{4}{1} = \frac{4}{2} = 2$. The unit rate is two miles per hour.

<u>Example</u>

A one pound box of cereal costs $3.20. Calculate the unit price in dollars per ounce

There are sixteen ounces in a pound, so ratio of the price of cereal to its weight can be written as $\frac{\$3.20}{16\text{ oz}}$. To determine the unit price, find the equivalent ratio which compares the price of the cereal to one ounce. To simplify the ratio, divide both the numerator and denominator by 16. Since $\frac{3.20 \div 16}{16 \div 16} = \frac{0.20}{1}$, the unit price of the cereal is twenty cents per ounce.

<u>Example</u>

A bag of 20 cough drops costs $1.68, and a bag of 50 cough drops costs $4.20. Determine which is a better deal

To determine which is the better deal, first find the unit prices of the products. For a bag of 20 cough drops at $1.68, the unit price is $\frac{\$1.68}{20\text{ cough drops}} = \frac{\$0.084}{1\text{ cough drop}}$, or 8.4 cents per cough drop. For a bag of 50 cough drops at $4.20, the unit price is $\frac{\$4.20}{50\text{ cough drops}} = \frac{\$0.084}{1\text{ cough drop}}$, or 8.4 cents per cough drop. Neither bag is a better bargain than the other since both cost the same amount per cough drop.

<u>Example</u>

Determine what it means for two quantities to have a proportional relationship.

When two quantities have a proportional relationship, there exists a constant of proportionality between the quantities; the product of this constant and one of the quantities is equal to the other quantity. For example, if one lemon costs $0.25, two lemons cost $0.50, and three lemons cost $0.75, there is a proportional relationship

- 16 -

between the total cost of lemons and the number of lemons purchased. The constant of proportionality is the unit price, namely $0.25/lemon. Notice that the total price of lemons, t, can be found by multiplying the unit price of lemons, p, and the number of lemons, n: $t = pn$.

Determining whether two quantities have a proportional relationship in a graph

If two quantities are graphed on the coordinate plane, and the result is a straight line through the origin, then the two quantities are proportional.

<u>Example</u>

For the graphs below, determine whether there exists a proportional relationship between x and y. If a proportional relationship exists, find the constant of proportionality and write an equation for the line.

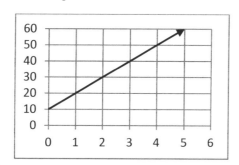

Though the graph of the relationship between x and y is a straight line, it does not pass through the origin. So, though y varies directly as x, the ratio $\frac{y}{x}$ is not constant: for instance, $\frac{20}{1} \neq \frac{30}{2} \neq \frac{40}{3}$..

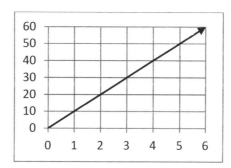

The graph of a proportional relationship is a straight line through the origin.

This graph is a straight line through the origin, so the relationship between x and y is proportional. The constant of proportionality is represented by the ratio $\frac{y}{x}$. This constant is the same as the unit rate. The constant of proportionality is equal to the y-value when $x = 1$. Since the ratio $\frac{y}{x}$ is 10 (see that $\frac{y}{x} = \frac{10}{1} = \frac{20}{2} = \frac{30}{3}$ and so on), or since $y = 10$ when $x = 1$, the constant of proportionality is 10. The relationship between x and y is represented by the equation $y = 10x$.

Determining whether two quantities have a proportional relationship given a table of values

If the ratio of y to x is constant for all values of x and y besides zero, then there is a proportional relationship between the two variables. The value $\frac{y}{x}$ is the constant of proportionality.

Example

Determine whether there exists a proportional relationship between x and y. If a proportional relationship exists, find the constant of proportionality and write an equation to represent the relationship.

x	1	2	3	4
y	5	9	13	17

If the ratio of y to x is constant for all values of x and y besides zero, then there is a proportional relationship between the two variables. The value $\frac{y}{x}$ is the constant of proportionality.

The ratio of y to x is not constant; therefore, the values in the table do not represent a proportional relationship:

x	1	2	3	4
y	5	9	13	17
$\frac{y}{x}$	$\frac{5}{1} = 5$	$\frac{9}{2} = 4.5$	$\frac{13}{3} = 4.\overline{3}$	$\frac{17}{4} = 4.25$

Example

Determine whether there exists a proportional relationship between x and y. If a proportional relationship exists, find the constant of proportionality and write an equation to represent the relationship.

x	1	2	3	4
y	1	4	9	16

If the ratio of y to x is constant for all values of x and y besides zero, then there is a proportional relationship between the two variables. The value $\frac{y}{x}$ is the constant of proportionality.

The ratio of y to x is not constant; therefore, the values in the table do not represent a proportional relationship:

x	1	2	3	4
y	1	4	9	16
$\frac{y}{x}$	$\frac{1}{1} = 1$	$\frac{4}{2} = 2$	$\frac{9}{3} = 3$	$\frac{16}{4} = 4$

<u>Example</u>

Determine whether there exists a proportional relationship between x and y. If a proportional relationship exists, find the constant of proportionality and write an equation to represent the relationship.

x	1	2	3	4
y	2.5	5	7.5	10

If the ratio of y to x is constant for all values of x and y besides zero, then there is a proportional relationship between the two variables. The value $\frac{y}{x}$ is the constant of proportionality.

The ratio of y to x is 2.5; therefore, the values in the table represent the proportional relationship modeled by the equation $y = 2.5x$:

x	1	2	3	4
y	2.5	5	7.5	10
$\frac{y}{x}$	$\frac{2.5}{1} = 2.5$	$\frac{5}{2} = 2.5$	$\frac{7.5}{3} = 2.5$	$\frac{10}{4} = 2.5$

<u>Example</u>

Suppose gasoline costs \$3 per gallon. Create a table of values for the total cost of gasoline and the gallons of gasoline purchased.

The graph is confined to the first-quadrant of the coordinate plane because neither the amount of gas nor the price of the gas can be negative. Since the cost depends on the number of gallons purchased, plot the number of gallons along the horizontal axis and the cost along the vertical axis.

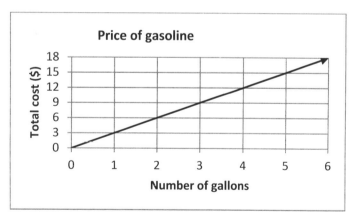

<u>Example</u>

Create a graph of the relationship between the total cost and the gallons of gasoline purchased

The graph is confined to the first-quadrant of the coordinate plane because neither the amount of gas nor the price of the gas can be negative. Since the cost depends on

- 19 -

the number of gallons purchased, plot the number of gallons along the horizontal axis and the cost along the vertical axis.

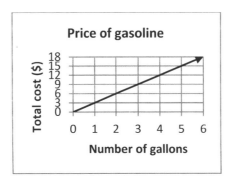

Write an equation which relates total cost to gallons of gasoline purchased.

The equation for the line is y=3x, or total cost=3×number of gallons purchased.

Example

Find the rate of travel from a graph representing a proportional relationship between travel time in hours (graphed along the horizontal axis) and distance traveled in miles (graphed along the vertical axis).

The slope of the line represents the rate of travel, or the proportionality constant, in miles per hour. The slope of a line is its vertical change, or rise, divided by its horizontal change, or run. These values can be determined from by counting the vertical and horizontal distances between any two points on the line or by using the equation $\frac{y_2-y_1}{x_2-x_1}$, where (x_1, y_1) and (x_2, y_2) are points on the line.

A point on the line shows the distance traveled at a particular travel time. Since the ratio of distance to time is constant along the graph representing a proportion relationship, any point on the graph can be used to find the rate by simply finding the ratio of y to x. For example, a point (3,90) on the graph indicates that it takes three hours to travel ninety miles, so the rate is $\frac{90\ miles}{3\ hours}$= 30 miles per hour.

Since the unit rate, miles per hour, compares the distance traveled in miles to one hour, the unit rate is the y-coordinate when x=1. For example, if the line passes through (1,30), the rate is 30 miles per hour.

Using proportions to solve percent problems

A proportion is a statement of equivalence between two ratios. In percent problems, both ratios compare parts to a whole; in particular, a percentage expresses parts per 100. A proportion which can be used to solved a percent problem is $\frac{part}{whole} = \frac{percent}{100}$.

In the given scenario, 4 is 80% of some number a, so 4 represents part of the unknown number. The proportion, therefore, is $\frac{4}{a} = \frac{80}{100}$. There are many ways to solve proportions. Notice that $\frac{80}{100}$ reduces to $\frac{4}{5}$, so $a = 5$.

<u>Example</u>

A family of six dines at a restaurant which charges an automatic gratuity for parties of six or more. A tip of $28 is added to their bill of $80. Determine the percent gratuity charged.

One way to determine the percent gratuity charged is to set up and solve a proportion of the form

$$\frac{part}{whole} = \frac{percent}{100}.$$

$$\frac{28}{80} = \frac{p}{100}$$

There are many ways to solve proportions. Notice that $\frac{28}{80}$ reduces to $\frac{7}{20}$, which can easily be converted to a fraction with a denominator of 100 by multiplying the numerator and denominator by 5.

$$\frac{7 \times 5}{20 \times 5} = \frac{35}{100}$$

So, $p = 35$. The gratuity added is 35%.

<u>Example</u>

The ratio of flour to sugar in a cookie recipe is 3:1. Find the amount of sugar needed for 1 ½ cups of flour

There are many ways to solve this problem using proportional reasoning. One way is to notice that the amount of flour divided by three gives the amount of sugar.

cups of flour: cups of sugar

$$\overset{\div 3}{\frown}$$
$$3{:}1$$

So, the amount of sugar needed for 1 ½ cups of flour can be found by dividing $1\frac{1}{2}$ by 3. $1\frac{1}{2} \div 3 = \frac{3}{2} \times \frac{1}{3} = \frac{3}{6} = \frac{1}{2}$.

$$\overset{\div 3}{\frown}$$
$$1\frac{1}{2} : \frac{1}{2}$$

- 21 -

The amount of sugar needed is ½ cup.

Example

Suppose you purchase a $7.00 entrée and a $2.00 drink at your favorite restaurant.

- Determine the amount of a 10% tax on your purchase.
- Determine the amount of a 15% tip on the pre-tax amount.
- Find the total price of the meal, including tax and tip.

The amount of your purchase before tax and tip is $9.00. There are many way to calculate the amount of tax on the purchase. One method is to set up and solve a proportion:

The amount of the tax will be calculated as a fraction of the purchase price. That fraction comparing the tax amount to the pre-tax price is equal to 10%, or $\frac{10}{100}$. So, $\frac{tax\ amount}{\$9.00} = \frac{10}{100}$. A tax amount of $0.90 satisfies the proportion.

Another method involves translating the problem into a mathematical expression which represents the tax amount, which is *10% of the purchase.*

A percent is a ratio out of 100, so $10\% = \frac{10}{100} = 0.10$.

The word "of" indicates multiplication.

The purchase price is $9.

So, *10% of the purchase* translates to $0.10 \times \$9$, which equals $0.90.

Again, there are many ways to calculate the amount of the tip. 15% of $9.00 translates to 0.15×$9, which equals $1.35.

The total price is the cost of the meal plus the tax plus the tip: $9.00+$0.90+$1.35=$11.25.

Example

A number is decreased by 20%. The resulting number is then increased by 20%. Determine whether the consequent number is greater than, less than, or equal to the original number

If a number is decreased by 20%, and the resulting number is increased by 20%, then the consequent number will be less than the original number.

Consider, for instance, that the original number is 100.

20% of 100 is $0.20 \times 100 = 20$, and $100 - 20 = 80$.

20% of 80 is $0.20 \times 80 = 16$, and $80 + 16 = 96$.

96 is less than 100.

<u>Example</u>

A school has 400 students; 220 of these students are girls. If the ratio of boys to girls in a class of twenty is representative of the ratio of boys to girls school-wide, determine how many boys are in the class.

Since the ratio of boys to girls in the class is equal to the ratio of boys to girls in the school, the ratio of boys to students in the class must also equal to the ratio of boys to students in the school.

$$\frac{Number\ of\ boys\ in\ the\ school}{number\ of\ students\ in\ the\ school} = \frac{number\ of\ boys\ in\ the\ class}{number\ of\ students\ in\ the\ class}$$

In a school of 400 students, 220 of which are girls, there are $400 - 220 = 180$ boys. The ratio of boys to total students is 180/400, which reduces to 9/20. So, in the class of twenty students, there must be nine boys.

Check to see that the ratio of boys to girls in the class is indeed equal to ratio school-wide. If there are nine boys in a class of twenty, then there are eleven girls:

$$\frac{9\ boys}{11\ girls} = \frac{180\ boys}{220\ girls}$$

One way to determine whether or not this statement is true is to cross multiply. If the products are equal, then so are the ratios.

$$9 \times 220 = 1980$$

$$11 \times 180 = 1980$$

<u>Example</u>

Use a number line to find the sum of 2.1 and 3.2.

Plot 2.1 on a number line and move three and two tenths spaces to the right.

Additive inverse

The sum of a number and its additive inverse, or opposite, is the additive identity, 0.

<u>Example</u>

Find the additive inverse of

3

-5

x

The additive inverse of 3 is -3 because $3 + (-3) = 0$.

The additive inverse of -5 is 5 because $-5 + 5 = 0$.

- 23 -

The additive inverse of x is $-x$ because $x + (-x) = 0$.

Multiplicative inverse

The product of a number and its multiplicative inverse is the multiplicative identity, 1. The multiplicative inverse of a number is also called its reciprocal. The reciprocal of a non-zero rational number is also rational. Zero does not have a multiplicative because the product of zero and any number is zero and can therefore not equal 1 and because zero can never be in the denominator of a fraction.

Example

Find the multiplicative inverse of

5

$-\dfrac{2}{3}$

x such that $x \neq 0$.

The multiplicative inverse of 5 is $\dfrac{1}{5}$ because $5\left(\dfrac{1}{5}\right) = 1$.

The multiplicative inverse of $-\dfrac{2}{3}$ is $-\dfrac{3}{2}$ because $-\dfrac{2}{3}\left(-\dfrac{3}{2}\right) = 1$.

The multiplicative inverse of x is $\dfrac{1}{x}$ when $x \neq 0$ because $x\left(\dfrac{1}{x}\right) = 1$ when $x \neq 0$.

Example

An atom of oxygen has eight positively charged protons and eight negatively charged electrons

- Determine the charge of an atom of oxygen.
- When an atom gains or loses electrons, it becomes an ion. Determine the charge of an oxygen ion which contains two more electrons than an oxygen atom.

An atom of oxygen has a charge of zero because it has the same number of positively charged protons as it does negatively charged electrons: $8 + (-8) = 0$.

An oxygen ion has a charge of -2 because the neutral atom has gained two negatively charged electrons: $0 + (-2) = -2$ or $8 + (-10) = -2$.

<u>Example</u>

Using number lines, show that 2 ½ − 2 ½ = 2 ½ + (−2 ½) = −2 ½ + 2 ½ = 0.

To subtract 2 ½ from 2 ½ on a number line, start at 2 ½ and move two and a half spaces to the left.

$$2 ½ − 2 ½ = 0$$

To simplify 2 ½ + (−2 ½) on a number line, start at 2 ½ and move two and a half spaces to the left. 2 ½ + (−2 ½) = 0.

Notice that adding -2 ½ to 2 ½ is that same subtracting 2 ½ from 2 ½.

To add 2 ½ to -2 ½ on a number line, start at -2 ½ and move two and a half spaces to the right.   −2 ½ + 2 ½ = 0

As always, the sum of a number and its opposite is zero.

$$2 ½ − 2 ½ = 2 ½ + (−2 ½) = −2 ½ + 2 ½ = 0$$

<u>Example</u>

Express each as a positive or negative number. Then, write a phrase to represent the number's opposite.

- A gain of four yards
- A deduction of ten points
- A 5°F drop in temperature
- A debit of $1.60
- An extra half-mile

A gain of four yards → **+4** yards. The opposite is *a loss of four yards*, or **−4** yards.

A deduction of ten points → **−10** points. The opposite is *an addition of 10 points*, or **+10** points.

A 5°F drop in temperature → **−5°F**. The opposite is *an increase in temperature of 5°F*, or **+5°F**.

A debit of $1.60→ **−$1.60**. The opposite is *a credit of $1.60*, or **+$1.60**.

An extra half-mile→ **+½** mile. The opposite is *a half-mile less*, or **−½** mile

Absolute value

The absolute value of a number is the number's distance from zero on a number line. A measure of distance is always positive, so absolute value is always positive.

Example

Show that $|3|=|-3|$.

The absolute value of 3, written as $|3|$, is 3 because the distance between 0 and 3 on a number line is three units. Likewise, the absolute value of -3, written as $|-3|$, is 3 because the distance between 0 and -3 on a number line is three units. So, $|3|=|-3|$.

Multiplying and dividing positive and negative numbers

The product or quotient of two positive numbers is positive.

$$2 \times 4 = 8$$

$$18 \div 3 = 6$$

The product or quotient of two negative numbers is positive.

$$(-3)(-1) = 3$$

$$\frac{-18}{-9} = 2$$

The product or quotient of a positive and a negative number or a negative and a positive number is negative.

$$4(-2) = -8$$

$$-3 \times 6 = -18$$

$$\frac{20}{-10} = -2$$

$$-15 \div 3 = -5$$

Example

For integers p and q, $q \neq 0$, $-\left(\frac{p}{q}\right) = \frac{-p}{q} = \frac{p}{-q}$. Illustrate this property using an example.

Choose an integer value for p and a non-zero integer value for q to show that $-\left(\frac{p}{q}\right) = \frac{-p}{q} = \frac{p}{-q}$. For instance, when p=10 and q=2,

$$-\left(\frac{p}{q}\right) = -\left(\frac{10}{2}\right) = -5$$

$$\frac{-p}{q} = \frac{-10}{2} = -5$$

$$\frac{p}{-q} = \frac{10}{-2} = -$$

Example

A jacket is marked 75% off. Determine which of these methods will give the discounted price of the jacket.

- Find 75% of the jacket's original price and subtract the result from the original price.
- Find 25% of the jacket's original price.
- Divide the original price by four.

All of these methods will give the discounted price of the jacket. If x is the jacket's original price, its new price is $x - 0.75x$. This expression simplifies to $0.25x$. $0.25 = \frac{25}{100} = \frac{1}{4}$, so 0.25x can be rewritten as $\frac{1}{4}x$, which equals $\frac{x}{4}$.

Example

A person plans to lose ½ pound each week by following a healthy diet. Write and simplify an expression to show his expected weight loss after six weeks of healthy eating

A loss of ½ pound each week for six weeks translates to $\left(-\frac{1}{2}\right)(6)$, which simplifies to -3. He can expect to lose three pounds in six weeks.

Example

A gymnast's routine has a start value of 16 points. During her routine, she incurs three deductions of one-tenth of a point, two deductions of three-tenths of a point, and one deduction of half a point. Determine the score she receives for her performance.

Write an expression to represent the gymnast's score. Each deduction is subtracted from her start value. Write all the deductions as fractions or as decimals. $\frac{1}{10} = 0.1; \frac{3}{10} = 0.3; \frac{1}{2} = 0.5$.

$$16 - 3(0.1) - 2(0.3) - 0.5$$

$$16 - 0.3 - 0.6 - 0.5$$

$$15.7 - 0.6 - 0.5$$

$$15.1 - 0.5 = 14.6$$

The gymnast's score is 14.6.

- 27 -

<u>Example</u>

A service provider charges $25.75 for phone, $27.75 for internet, and $33.50 for cable each month. A one-time credit of $35.50 is applied towards a customer's bill when the customer opts to prepay for service by quarterly bank draft. After a new customer orders phone, internet, and cable service and signs up for automatic bill pay, she notices a transaction on her bank statement of -$225.50. Write an expression which justifies this charge made by the service provider.

If the customer pays her bill quarterly, then she pays for three months of service at one time. So, her bill includes three times the total for the phone charge and the internet charge and the cable charge. A credit of $35.00 is given only once.

$$3[(-\$25.75) + (-\$27.75) + (-\$33.50)] + \$35.00$$

$$= 3(-\$87.00) + \$35.50$$

$$= -\$261.00 + \$35.50$$

$$= -\$225.50$$

Commutative property of addition and multiplication

The commutative property of addition states that the order in which two numbers are added does not change their sum; the commutative property of multiplication states that the order in which two numbers are multiplied does not change their product.

$$a + b = b + a$$

$$ab = ba$$

Associative property of addition and multiplication

The associate property of addition states that a series of added numbers can be grouped in various ways without affecting the sum; the associative property of multiplication states that a series of multiplied numbers can be grouped in various ways without affecting the product.

$$a + (b + c) = (a + b) + c$$

$$a(bc) = (ab)c$$

Additive identity and the multiplicative identity

The additive identity is the number which can be added to a number without changing its value; that number is zero. The multiplicative identity is the number which can be multiplied by a number without changing its value; that number is one.

<u>Example</u>

Use the distributive property to simplify $-\frac{1}{2}(x - 8)$.

The distributive property states that $a(b + c) = ab + ac$ and $a(b - c) = ab - ac$.

$$-\frac{1}{2}(x - 8) = \left(-\frac{1}{2}\right)(x) - \left(-\frac{1}{2}\right)(8) = -\frac{1}{2}x + 4.$$

- 28 -

<u>Example</u>

Name the property used in each step of simplifying $\frac{3}{4} \cdot \frac{2}{3} + \frac{3}{4} \cdot \frac{1}{3}$.

$$\frac{3}{4} \cdot \frac{2}{3} + \frac{3}{4} \cdot \frac{1}{3} = \frac{3}{4}\left(\frac{2}{3} + \frac{1}{3}\right)$$

$$\frac{3}{4}\left(\frac{2}{3} + \frac{1}{3}\right) = \frac{3}{4}(1)$$

$$\frac{3}{4}(1) = \frac{3}{4}$$

$\frac{3}{4} \cdot \frac{2}{3} + \frac{3}{4} \cdot \frac{1}{3} = \frac{3}{4}\left(\frac{2}{3} + \frac{1}{3}\right)$ Distributive property

$\frac{3}{4}\left(\frac{2}{3} + \frac{1}{3}\right) = \frac{3}{4}(1)$ Substitution property of equality

(Since $\frac{2}{3} + \frac{1}{3} = 1$, the number 1 can replace the expression $\frac{2}{3} + \frac{1}{3}$.)

$\frac{3}{4}(1) = \frac{3}{4}$ Multiplicative identity

<u>Example</u>

Simplify.

$$-\frac{2}{3}\left(a - \frac{1}{4}\right)$$

$$\left(\frac{3}{4}x + 4\right) + \left(\frac{1}{4}x - 3\right)$$

Use the distributive property to simplify $-\frac{2}{3}\left(a - \frac{1}{4}\right)$.

$$-\frac{2}{3}\left(a - \frac{1}{4}\right) = -\frac{2}{3} \cdot a + \left(-\frac{2}{3}\right)\left(-\frac{1}{4}\right)$$

$$= -\frac{2}{3}a + \frac{2}{12}$$

$$= -\frac{2}{3}a + \frac{1}{6}$$

Use the associative and commutative properties of addition to simplify $\left(\frac{3}{4}x + 4\right) + \left(\frac{1}{4}x - 3\right)$.

- 29 -

$$\left(\frac{3}{4}x + 4\right) + \left(\frac{1}{4}x - 3\right) = \frac{3}{4}x + 4 + \frac{1}{4}x - 3$$

$$= \frac{3}{4}x + \frac{1}{4}x + 4 - 3$$

$$= x + 1$$

<u>Example</u>

Factor $\frac{1}{2}$ from the expression $\frac{1}{4}x - \frac{1}{2}$.

To factor $\frac{1}{2}$ from the expression $\frac{1}{4}x - \frac{1}{2}$, divide each term in the expression by $\frac{1}{2}$.

$$\frac{1}{4}x \div \frac{1}{2} = \frac{1}{4} \cdot x \cdot \frac{2}{1} = \frac{1}{4} \cdot \frac{2}{1} \cdot x = \frac{2}{4} \cdot x = \frac{1}{2}x$$

$$-\frac{1}{2} \div \frac{1}{2} = -1$$

The factored expression is $\frac{1}{2}\left(\frac{1}{2}x - 1\right)$.

Words and/or phrases

<u>Addition</u>

Some words and phrases that indicate addition are sum, plus, total, and, increased by, more, together, added to, combined with, gain.

<u>Subtraction</u>

Some words and phrases that indicate subtraction are difference, minus, less, decreased by, take away, fewer than, from, subtracted from, loss.

<u>Multiplication</u>

Some words and phrases that indicate multiplication are product, times, multiplied by, of, twice/double (×2), thrice/triple (×3).

<u>Division</u>

Some words and phrases that indication division are quotient, divided by, into, among, between, over, per, for every, ratio of, out of.

These lists are not exhaustive.

<u>Example</u>

Joshua calculates that the product of $19\frac{3}{4}$ and $10\frac{1}{4}$ is $404\frac{7}{8}$. Use mental estimation to determine the reasonableness of his answer.

The product of two numbers is found by multiplying those numbers, so the product of $19\frac{3}{4}$ and $10\frac{1}{4}$ is about 200 since $19\frac{3}{4}$ is close to 20 and $10\frac{1}{4}$ is close to 10. An answer of $404\frac{7}{8}$ seems unreasonable, so Joshua should check his calculation.

- 30 -

Example

Suppose you wish to center a 3 ¼ ft wide painting over a buffet which is 5 ¾ ft wide. Approximate how far each edge of the painting would be from each edge of the buffet.

The painting is just over 3 ft wide, and the buffet is just under 6 feet wide. So, the difference in the width of the buffet and the painting is about 3 ft.. The painting is centered above the buffet, half of the difference in width will be space to the left of the painting and the other half will be space to the right of the painting. Half of 3 ft is 1 ½ ft. So, each edge of the painting should be about 1 ½ ft from each edge of the buffet.

Mathematical symbols

= equals, is equal to, is, was, were, will be, yields, is the same as, amounts to, becomes

>**is** greater than, **is** more than

≥ **is** greater than or equal to, **is** at least, is no less than

<**is** less than, **is** fewer than

≤ **is** less than or equal to, **is** at most, is no more than

Example

Write three sentences which would translate into the inequality $2(x + 4) \geq 6$.

There are many ways to write $2(x + 4) \geq 6$ as a sentence, including

Two times the sum of a number and four is greater than or equal to six.

Twice the quantity x increased by four is at least six.

The product of two and a number to which four has been added must be no less than six.

Example

An $80 dress is marked down 25%. Find the price of the dress after the discount.

One way to find the price of the dress after the discount is to calculate the amount of the discount and subtract it from the price of the dress:

The amount of the discount is 25% of $80, or $0.25 \times \$80 = \$20$.

The price of the dress after the discount is $\$80 - \$20 = \$60$.

Another way to find the discounted price is to write, simplify, and evaluate an expression representing the problem:

- If p = original price, then $0.25p$ represents the amount of the discount. So, an expression for the new price of the dress is $p - 0.25p$, which simplifies to $0.75p$. In other words, the discounted price of the dress is 75% of the original price. $0.75p = 0.75(\$80) = \$60$.

- 31 -

<u>Example</u>

If px represents the price of an item, write an expression can be used to find

- The price of the item with 8% sales tax.
- The pre-tax price of the item during a half-off sale.
- The after-tax price of the item during a half-off sale.

The amount of an 8% sales tax added to an item which costs px dollars is $0.08p$. The price of the item with the sales tax is $p + 0.08p$, which simplifies to $\mathbf{1.08p}$.

If the item is half off, the amount of the discount is $\frac{1}{2}p$. The new price of the item is the original price minus the discount, or $-\frac{1}{2}p$, which simplifies to $\frac{1}{2}\boldsymbol{p}$.

The price of the half-off item with 8% sales tax is $1.08\left(\frac{1}{2}p\right) = 1.08(0.5p) = \mathbf{0.54p}$.

Determining the order of operations used to simplify expressions

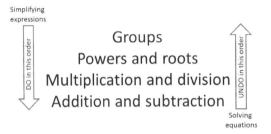

When simplifying an expression, work first within groups, which can be found within grouping symbols such as parentheses but also can be found under radical signs, in numerators or denominators of fractions, as exponents, etc. without such grouping symbols. Next, simplify powers and roots. Then multiply and divide from left to right; finally, add and subtract from left to right.

<u>Relate this to the sequence of operations used when solving equations</u>

When solving an equation, it is often helpful to first use order of operations to simplify the expressions on both sides of the equation, if possible. Then, undo the operations which have been performed on the variable by using inverse operations in reverse order of operations.

<u>Example</u>

Alina spent $20 at the fair. She paid $2 for admission plus $1.50 for every ride. Write and solve an equation to determine how many rides she rode.

Let x = the number of rides Alina rode at the fair. The expression $\$1.50x$ represents the amount of money spent riding rides. Alina spent a total of $\$1.50x + \$2$ on rides and admission; this amount equals $20, so

$$\$1.50x + \$2 = \$20$$

$$\underline{ -\$2 -\$2}$$

$$\$1.50x + \$0 = \$18$$

$$\frac{\$1.50x}{\$1.50} = \frac{\$18}{\$1.50}$$

$$x = 12$$

Alina rode twelve rides at the fair.

Example

24 feet of fencing was used to enclose a rectangular garden with a width of 8 feet. Write and solve an equation to determine the length of the garden.

The perimeter of a rectangle can be found using the expression $2l + 2w$, where l is the rectangle's length and w is its width. The perimeter of the garden is 24 feet, and the width of the garden is 8 feet, so

$$2l + 2(8) = 24$$

$$2l + 16 = 24$$

$$\underline{ -16 -16}$$

$$2l + 0 = 8$$

$$\frac{2l}{2} = \frac{8}{2}$$

$$l = 4$$

The length of the garden is 4 feet.

Example

Leng receives a weekly allowance of five dollars when he completes his usual chores. He can earn an additional fifty cents for each additional chore he does. Write and solve an inequality to find the number of extra chores he should do to earn at least ten dollars this week.

Let n = the number of extra chores Leng must complete. For every extra chore, he earns $0.50, so $0.5n$ represents the amount of money, in dollars, he will earn from the extra chores. The total amount of money he earns in dollars is represented by the expressions $0.5n + 5$. This week, he wishes to earn at least $10, so he wants to either earn $10 or more than $10. Thus, the inequality $5 + 0.5n \geq 10$ represents this scenario.

$$0.5n + 5 \geq 10$$

$$\underline{ -5 -5}$$

$$0.5n + 0 \geq 5$$

- 33 -

$$\frac{0.5}{0.5} n \geq \frac{5}{0.5}$$

$$n \geq 10$$

Leng must complete at least 10 extra chores to earn $10 or more.

Example

On a map, the distance between two cities measures 2 ½ inches. A distance of one inch on the map represents an actual distance of 30 miles. Find the actual distance between the two cities.

Use proportional reasoning to find the distance between the two cities. One way to set up a proportion from the given information is to equate two ratios which compare inches to miles, where x represents the unknown distance between the two cities in miles.

$$\frac{2\frac{1}{2}}{x} = \frac{1}{30}$$

There are many ways to solve a proportion. One way is to cross-multiply.

$$2\frac{1}{2} \times 30 = x \times 1$$

$$\frac{5}{2} \times \frac{30}{1} = x$$

$$\frac{150}{2} = x$$

$$75 = x$$

The distance between the cities is 75 miles.

Example

A room has dimensions of 12' wide by 15' long. Using a scale of 1/4":1', draw a blueprint of the room.

First, determine the dimensions of the room on the blueprint. Let w represent the width in inches and l represent the length in inches of the room on the scale drawing.

$$\frac{\frac{1}{4} \text{ in}}{1 \text{ ft}} = \frac{w}{12 \text{ ft}}$$

Using cross-multiplication, $1 \cdot w = \left(\frac{1}{4}\right)(12) = 3$. The width of the room on the blueprint is 3 in.

$$\frac{\frac{1}{4} \text{ in}}{1 \text{ ft}} = \frac{l}{15 \text{ ft}}$$

Again using cross-multiplication, $1 \cdot l = \left(\frac{1}{4}\right)(15) = \frac{15}{4} = 3\frac{3}{4}$. The length of the room on the blueprint is $3\frac{3}{4}$ in.

Example

Below is a box drawn at 1:4 scale.

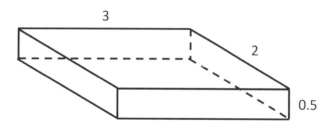

Draw the box at a scale of 1:8.

Determine the actual dimensions of the box.

A scale of 1:4 mean that each side of the box is $\frac{1}{4}$ the size of the actual box.

Redrawing at a scale of 1:8 means that each side of the drawing will be $\frac{1}{8}$ the size of the actual box, or $\frac{1}{2}$ of the size of the given scale drawing since $\frac{1}{2} \times \frac{1}{4} = \frac{1}{8}$. So, draw a box whose dimensions are half of the length, width, and height of the given scale drawing. Since ½=0.5, use either number to calculate the new dimensions.
0.5 × 3 in = 1.5 in   0.5 × 2 in = 1 in   0.5 × 0.5 in = 0.25 in

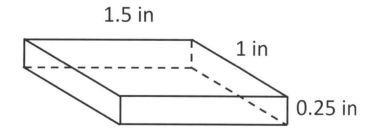

Since each side of the scale drawing is $\frac{1}{4}$ the size of each side of the actual box, the sides of the box are four times the size of the sides in the scale drawing. So, the box's actual dimensions are

4×3 in $= 12$ in 4×2 in $= 8$ in 4×0.5 in $= 2$ in.

Example

The ratio of the lengths of two squares is 1:5.

- Determine the ratio of the perimeters of the two squares.
- Determine the ratio of the areas of the two squares.

If the ratio of the lengths of two squares is 1:5, the ratio of the perimeters of the two squares is also 1:5. Consider, for instance, a square with a length of 1 cm. Its width would also be 1 cm, so it perimeter would be $2l + 2w = 2(1 \text{ cm}) + 2(1 \text{ cm}) = 2 \text{ cm} + 2 \text{ cm} = 4 \text{ cm}$. A square with a length five times that of the first square would have a perimeter of $2(5 \text{ cm}) + 2(5 \text{ cm}) = 10 \text{ cm} + 10 \text{ cm} = 20 \text{ cm}$. So, the ratio of the perimeters of the squares would be 4:20, which reduces to 1:5.

Considering the same two squares, the area of the first square would be $l \times w = (1 \text{ cm})(1 \text{ cm}) = 1 \text{ cm}^2$. The area of the second would be $(5 \text{ cm})(5 \text{ cm}) = 25 \text{ cm}^2$. So, the ratios of the areas of the squares **would be 1:25.**

Example

Determine whether or not a triangle can be constructed given

- The measures of three angles.
- The lengths of three sides.

The sum of the measures of a triangle's angles is always 180°. So, a triangle can be constructed from given angle measurements only if those measurements add to 180°.

The sum of the lengths of two shorter sides of a triangle must be greater than the length of the third side.

Example

Using a ruler and a protractor, draw a right triangle with the two shorter sides measuring 3 in and 4 in. Measure the length of the longest side and the approximate measures of the two non-right angles. Make sure the measurements are consistent with the properties of a triangle.

The length of the longest side is 5 inches. The angle across from the side measuring 4 inches is approximately 53°, and the other angle is approximately 37°. These measures are consistent with the properties of triangles:

- The sum of the angles of the triangle is $53° + 37° + 90° = 180°$. The combined lengths of the two shorter sides exceed the longest side: 3 in + 4 in > 5 *in*. The smallest angle forms the shortest side, and the largest angle forms the longest side.

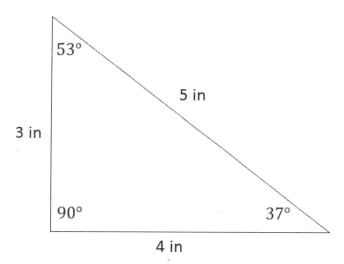

Example

An equilateral triangle whose sides each measure two inches is enlarged by a factor of four. Determine the measurements of the enlarged triangle's sides and angles.

A triangle which has three congruent sides also must have three congruent angles. Since the sum of the angles of a triangle is 180°, each angle measures $\frac{180°}{3} = 60°$. When a triangle is dilated, its angles remain the same; the lengths of the sides change but remain proportionally. Since the scale factor is four, the length of each the three sides is 2 in × 4 = 8 in. So, each angle of the enlarged triangle measures 60°, and each side measures 8 in.

<u>Example</u>

The area, A, of a parallelogram can be found using the formula $A = bh$, where b is the length of the base and h is the height, which is the distance between the parallelogram's base and its opposite, parallel side. Two congruent triangles are obtained when a parallelogram is cut in half from one of its corners to the opposite corner. From this information, determine the area formula of a triangle.

Two identical triangles make up the parallelogram's area, so the area of one triangle is half the area of the parallelogram. Since the area of a parallelogram is $A = bh$, the area of a triangle is $A = \frac{1}{2}bh$, where b is the base of the triangle and h is the height of the triangle as shown.

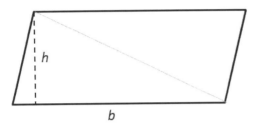 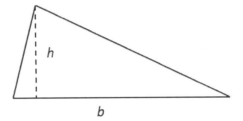

<u>Example</u>

Determine if no triangle, one triangle, or more than one triangle can be drawn given the side and/or angle measurements.

- Side lengths 3 cm, 4 cm, and 5 cm.
- Angle measurements 60°, 40°, and 80°.

In order to construct a triangle, the sum of the lengths of two shorter sides of a triangle must be greater than the length of the third side. $3 \text{ cm} + 4 \text{ cm} > 5 \text{ cm}$, so these sides can be used to draw one triangle.

The sum of the measures of a triangle's angles is always 180°. Since 60°+ 40°+ 80°=180°, a triangle can be constructed with these angle measurements. In fact, many similar triangles can be constructed with these angle measures.

<u>Example</u>

Determine the two-dimensional cross section obtained by slicing a right, triangular prism parallel to its base

A triangular prism contains two congruent triangular bases which lie in parallel planes. The side edges of a right prism are perpendicular to the base.

Taking the cross section of right, triangular prism parallel to its base yields a triangle which is congruent to the prism's base. One such cross section is illustrated.

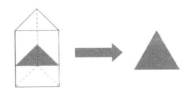

- 38 -

<u>Example</u>

Determine the two-dimensional cross section obtained by slicing a right, triangular prism perpendicular to its base

The cross section of right, triangular prism perpendicular to its base yields a rectangle. One such cross section is illustrated.

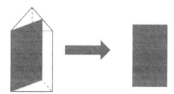

<u>Example</u>

Determine the two-dimensional cross section obtained by slicing a right, rectangular pyramid parallel to its base

A rectangular pyramid is one which has one rectangular base and four triangular sides which meet at an apex. The apex of a right pyramid lies directly above the center of the pyramid's base.

The cross section of a right, rectangular pyramid parallel to its base is a rectangle which is smaller than but similar to the rectangular base. One such cross section is illustrated.

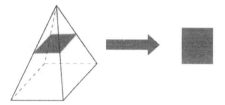

<u>Example</u>

Determine the two-dimensional cross section obtained by slicing a right, rectangular pyramid perpendicular to its base and through the apex.

A rectangular pyramid is one which has one rectangular base and four triangular sides which meet at an apex. The apex of a right pyramid lies directly above the center of the pyramid's base.

The cross section of a right, rectangular pyramid perpendicular to its base and through its apex is a triangle whose height is equal to the height of the pyramid. One such cross section is illustrated.

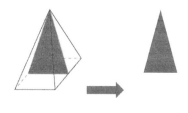

<u>Example</u>

Write the formulas used to find the circumference and area of a circle, respectively.

The formula used to find the circumference, C, of a circle is $C = 2\pi r$ or $C = \pi d$, where r is the radius of the circle and d its diameter. The formula used to find the area, A, of a circle is $A = \pi r^2$, where r is the radius of the circle.

<u>Example</u>

A round table has a diameter of 6 feet. A circular table cloth is cut from a piece of fabric in such a way that it hangs down 6 inches all the way around the table, and a decorative fringe is added along the cut. Using 3.14 as an approximation for π, determine the area of the table cloth and the length of the fringe. Round answers to the nearest tenth.

The area of the table cloth is found using the area formula of a circle, $A = \pi r^2$. First, find the radius of the table cloth.

Since the table cloth hangs down 6", which is equivalent to half a foot, add 0.5 ft to the radius of the table to find the radius of the table cloth. The radius of the table cloth is 3.5 ft, so the area of the table cloth is about 38.5 square feet:

$$A = \pi r^2$$

$$A = (3.14)(3.5 \text{ ft})^2$$

$$A = (3.14)(3.5 \text{ ft})^2$$

$$A = (3.14)(12.25 \text{ ft}^2) = 38.465 \text{ ft}^2$$

The fringe goes around the circular table cloth, so its length can be found using the formula for the circumference of a circle, $C = 2\pi r$. The length of the fringe is about 22.0 ft.

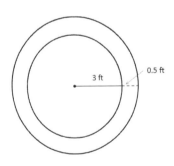

$$C = 2\pi r$$

$$C = 2(3.14)(3.5 \text{ ft}) = 21.98 \text{ ft}$$

Example

Name a pair of

Supplementary angles

Complementary angles

Vertical angles

Adjacent angles.

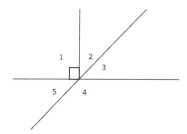

The sum of two supplementary angles is 180°. Angles 4 and 5 are supplementary, as are angles 3 and 4.

The sum of two complementary angles is 90°. Angles 2 and 3 are complimentary.

Vertical angles share a vertex but are not adjacent; rather, vertical angles are congruent angles across from each other in the X made by the intersection of two lines. Angles 3 and 5 are vertical angles.

Adjacent angles share a vertex and a side. Angles 1 and 2, 2 and 3, 3 and 4, 4 and 5, and 1 and 5 are adjacent.

Example

Solve for x and label each angle with its appropriate measure.

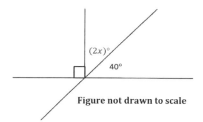

Figure not drawn to scale

Since the angle labeled $(2x)°$ is the complement to the 40° angle, the two add to 90°. So,

$$2x + 40 = 90$$
$$\underline{-40 \quad -40}$$
$$2x + 0 = 50$$
$$\frac{2x}{2} = \frac{50}{2}$$
$$x = 25$$

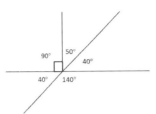

The angle labeled $(2x)°$ measures $(2 \times 25)° = 50°$.

The angle supplementary to the 40° angle must measure 140° since the sum of supplementary angles is 180°.

The angle across from the 40° angle is its vertical angle. Since vertical angles are congruent, that angle also measures 40°.

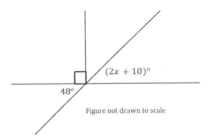

Figure not drawn to scale

Since the angle labeled $(2x)°$ is the complement to the 40° angle, the two add to 90°. So,

$$2x + 10 = 48$$
$$\underline{-10 \quad -10}$$
$$2x + 0 = 38$$
$$\frac{2x}{2} = \frac{38}{2}$$
$$x = 19$$

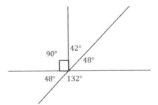

The angles label $(2x + 10)°$ measures 48°, so its complement measures $90° - 48° = 42°$, and its supplement measures $180° - 48° = 132°$.

Example

Match each measurement with the appropriate unit of measurement.

Length of a table
Area of a house   Units
Perimeter of a room   Feet
Surface area of a polyhedron   Square feet
                                         Cubic feet
Volume of a box

- 42 -

Distance between two houses
Storage capacity of a refrigerator

Lengths or distances are measured in units, while area is measured is square units and volume is measured in cubic units. When the unit of measure is feet:

- The length of a table is measured in *feet*.
- The area of a house is measured in *square feet*.
- The perimeter of a room is the distance around the room and is measured in *feet*.
- The surface area of a polyhedron is the sum of the areas of its polygonal faces and is measured in *square feet*.
- The volume of a box is measured in *cubic feet*.
- The distance between two houses is measured in *feet*.
- The storage capacity of a refrigerator is how much space is inside. The refrigerator's volume is measured in *cubic feet*.

<u>Example</u>

Find the surface area and volume of the box.

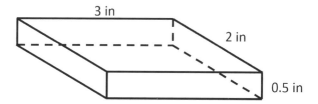

The surface area of a box is the sum of the areas of its six rectangular surfaces.

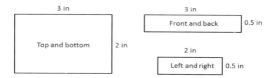

The area of the top rectangle is $A = lw = (3 \text{ in})(2 \text{ in}) = 6 \text{ in}^2$. The area of the top rectangle combined with the bottom rectangle is $6 \text{ in}^2 + 6 \text{ in}^2 = 12 \text{ in}^2$.

The area of the front rectangle is $A = lw = (3 \text{ in})(0.5 \text{ in}) = 1.5 \text{ in}^2$. The area of the front rectangle combined with the back rectangle is $1.5 \text{ in}^2 + 1.5 \text{ in}^2 = 3 \text{ in}^2$.

The area of the left side rectangle is $A = lw = (2 \text{ in})(0.5 \text{ in}) = 1 \text{ in}^2$. The area of the left and right side rectangles together is $1 \text{ in}^2 + 1 \text{ in}^2 = 2 \text{ in}^2$.

The total surface area of the box is $12 \text{ } in^2 + 3 \text{ } in^2 + 2 \text{ } in^2 = 17 \text{ } in^2$.

The volume, V, of a box is found by $V = lwh$. o, $V = (3 \text{ } in)(2 in)(0.5 \text{ } in) = 3 \text{ } in^3$.

<u>Example</u>

An 11'×13' room contains a 3' wide, 7' tall doorway and two 5'x3' windows. The ceiling height is 9'. Determine :

- The price to install baseboards which cost $1.25 per linear foot.
- The price to install flooring which costs $5 per square foot.
- If one gallon of paint which covers 400 square feet of surface is sufficient to paint the walls of the room.

Baseboards run along the edge of the room, but not across doorways. To determine the price for the baseboards, first determine how many feet are needed for the perimeter of the room, excluding the doorway. Use the formula for the perimeter of a rectangle to find the perimeter of the room: $2l + 2w = 2(11\ \text{ft}) + 2(13\ \text{ft}) = 48\ \text{ft}$. After adjusting for the width of the doorway, 45ft of baseboard is needed for the room. The price of baseboards is 45×1.25=$56.25.

To determine the price for flooring, first determine the area of the room. Use the formula for the area of a rectangle to find the area of the room: $lw = (11\ \text{ft})(13\ \text{ft}) = 143\ \text{ft}^2$. The price for the flooring is 143×5=$715.

To determine the amount of paint needed for the walls, first determine the total surface area to be covered. Two walls are 11'×9' and the other two walls are 13'×9'. Disregarding doors and windows, the total area of the walls is $2(11\ \text{ft})(9\ \text{ft}) + 2(13\ \text{ft})(9\ \text{ft}) = 198\ \text{ft}^2 + 234\ \text{ft}^2 = 432\ \text{ft}^2$. Take away the area of the door, which is $(3\ \text{ft})(7\ \text{ft}) = 21\ \text{ft}^2$, and the area of the windows, which is $2(5\ \text{ft})(3\ \text{ft}) = 30\ \text{ft}^2$: $432\ \text{ft}^2 - 21\ \text{ft}^2 - 30\ \text{ft}^2 = 381\ \text{ft}^2$. The amount of surface which needs paint is $381\ \text{ft}^2$. Purchasing one gallon of paint should be sufficient to cover the walls if only one coat of paint is needed.

<u>Example</u>

Find the perimeter of the shape below.

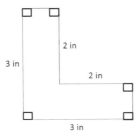

The perimeter of a polygon is the sum of its sides, which is 12 inches.

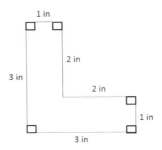

- 44 -

<u>Example</u>

Find the area of the shape below.

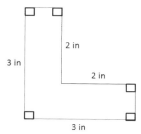

To find the area of an irregular polygon, draw it as a familiar polygon to which another familiar polygon is added or from which a familiar polygon is removed. For example, the shape can be viewed as vertically-oriented rectangle to which a horizontally-oriented rectangle is added, or it can be viewed as a square from which a smaller square is removed.

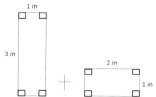
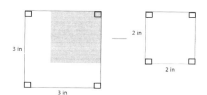

The area of the irregular polygon is the sum of the areas of the two rectangles shown. The area of a rectangle is $A = lw$, so the area of the polygon is $(3\text{ in})(1\text{ in}) + (2\text{ in})(1\text{ in}) = 3\text{ in}^2 + 2\text{ in}^2 = 5\text{ in}^2$.

The area of the irregular polygon is the area of the larger square minus the area of the smaller square. The larger square has side lengths of 3 inches, so the area is $(3\text{ in})(3\text{ in})=9\text{ in}^2$. The smaller square has an area of 4 in^2. So, the area of the irregular polygon is $9\text{ in}^2 - 4\text{ in}^2 = 5\text{ in}^2$.

Notice that either method of calculating the irregular polygon's area gives the same answer.

Mean, median, and mode

Mean, median, and mode are all measures of central tendency. Measures of central tendency summarize a set of data with values which represent the average, middle, or most common value. The mean, or average, of numerical data can be found by dividing the sum of the numbers in a set by how many numbers are in that set. When numerical data are organized from least to greatest, the middle number or average of the two middle numbers is the median of the set. The mode is the value which appears most frequently in a data set; there may be no mode, one mode, or more than one mode in a set.

<u>Example</u>

Find the mean, median, and mode of these numbers:

23, 42, 36, 21, 28, 29, 32, 28, 40, 36, 39.

The mean of a set of numbers is the sum of the numbers divided by how many numbers are in the set. So, the mean of this set of numbers is
$$\frac{23+42+36+21+28+29+32+28+40+36+39}{11} = \frac{354}{11} = 32.\overline{18}.$$

To find the median, put the numbers in increasing order and find the number in the middle:

21, 23, 28, 28, 29, **32**, 36, 36, 39, 40, 42. The median is 32.

The mode is the value in the set that occurs most frequently. There may be no mode, one mode, or more than one mode in a set. This set has two values that occur twice while all others occur only once. Thus, the modes are those two values, namely 28 and 36.

Random sampling

A random sample is a collection of members, chosen at random and with equal likelihood, from a group about which information is desired. Rather than collecting information from the entire group, which can be quite difficult when the group is very large, information is collected instead from the sample. If the sample is representative of the group and is sufficiently large, then the information gained from the sample is representative can be used to describe the group as a whole.

<u>Example</u>

Determine whether or not each represents a random sample of seventh graders at a middle school:

- A student selects all the seventh graders on her bus.
- A teacher puts the names of her first period students in a hat and draws ten names.
- A principal assigns uses a random number generator to select student ID numbers of seventh graders.

Each seventh grader must be chosen at random and must have an equal chance of being selected. Neither criterion is true in the first scenario. The teacher in the second scenario is selecting a random sample of students in her first period class, but this is not a random sample of the group of seventh graders as a whole. The principle's method of selecting is random and ensures that the likelihood of selecting one student is the same as the likelihood of selecting another.

- 46 -

Example

A random number generator produced the following sets of eight numbers between 1 and 99:

82, 60, 40, 69, 40, 36, 25, 59

98, 28, 15, 91, 51, 74, 11, 36

21, 66, 46, 16, 32, 73, 3, 81

91, 80, 32, 72, 1, 53, 51, 28.

Determine the mean of each set. Describe how well the mean of the each random sample represents the set from which the sample was taken.

The mean, or average, is a measure of central tendency which can be found by dividing the sum of the numbers in a set by how many numbers are in that set. The mean of the numbers 1 through 99 is 50, so the mean of a random sample of numbers taken from 1 to 99 should be approximately 50.

$$\frac{82 + 60 + 40 + 69 + 40 + 36 + 25 + 59}{8} = \frac{411}{8} = 51.375$$

$$\frac{98 + 28 + 15 + 91 + 51 + 74 + 11 + 36}{8} = \frac{404}{8} = 50.5$$

$$\frac{21 + 66 + 46 + 16 + 32 + 73 + 3 + 81}{9} = \frac{338}{8} = 42.25$$

$$\frac{91 + 80 + 32 + 72 + 1 + 53 + 51 + 28}{8} = \frac{408}{8} = 51$$

Samples 1, 2, and 4 seem to be a good representatives of the set from which they were taken. The mean of the values in the third sample varies more from the actual mean than the others. One way to improve the likelihood of a random sample's representation of the actual set is to collect more samples.

Example

Suppose all 567 seventh graders in a school vote on which field trip they would like to take from the following options: science center, art museum, or state capitol. Explain how an administrator might use the surveys to predict the most popular vote without tallying all of the results.

An administrator could compile the results from a random sample of surveys. For instance, if the surveys were shuffled, and 50 randomly chosen surveys showed a strong preference for the science center, then the administrator would likely predict that the science center will be the popular vote. To increase her confidence in the results, the administrator could increase the sample size by examining more surveys.

Example

> When determining the reading level of a book, a publisher considers many factors, including the average word length. Explain how a publisher might use random sampling to find the average word length in a book.

> To find the average word length in a book, a publisher might randomly select a set of words from the book and find the average length of those words. This average should be representative of the whole book if the words are indeed chosen at random.

Example

> The histogram below displays the heights of randomly selected eighteen-year-old boys and girls living in Atlanta, Georgia. Compare the variability within each group and between the groups.

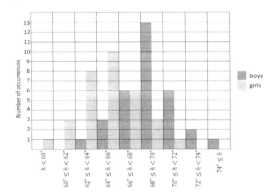

> Both of the histograms show a similar, normal distribution of heights, with fewer individuals at the two extremes and the majority clustered at a more central point. The two distributions overlap, which means that some eighteen-year-old boys are the same height as some eighteen-year-old girls. However, there is a noticeable shift to the right in the bell-shaped distributions for boys when compared to girls; this indicates that eighteen-year-old boys are generally taller than girls of the same age. According to the chart, the most common height for eighteen-year-old boys is between 68 and 70 inches, while the most common height among girls is 64 and 66 inches.

Explain what each of the probabilities means in terms of the likelihood of an event:

$$0$$

$$\frac{1}{100,000}$$

$$\frac{1}{2}$$

$$99\%$$

$$1$$

- 48 -

The probability of an event occurring ranges from 0 to 1 when expressed as a fraction or decimal and between 0% and 100% when expressed as a percentage. When there are a finite number of outcomes, a probability of 0 means that the occurrence of an event is impossible, while a probability of 1 means the occurrence is certain. The closer a value is to 0, the less likely it is to occur. For example, a probability of $\frac{1}{100,000}$ indicates that an event is unlikely to occur, whereas a probability of 99% indicates a likely event. Since ½ is halfway between 0 and 1, a probability of ½, or 50%, means that an event is neither likely nor unlikely.

In terms of probability, define and give an example of a

- Sample space
- Simple event
- Compound event

The set of all outcomes of a probability experiment is called the sample space. For example, if a coin is tossed one time, there are two possible outcomes: heads or tails. So, the sample space consists of two elements. If a coin is tossed two times, there are four possible outcomes: heads then tails, heads then heads, tails then heads, tails then tails. So, the sample space consists of four outcomes.

A simple event consists of only one outcome in the sample space. For instance, the event of getting heads in a single coin toss is a simple event.

Compound events consist of more than one outcome in the sample space. For instance, the event of getting heads at least once in two coin tosses is a compound event. The compound event of getting heads is composed of three outcomes: heads then tails, heads then heads, tails then heads.

Determine the following:

- The probability of winning a single coin toss.
- The probability of a rolling a multiple of 3 on a die.
- The probability of randomly picking a green marble from a bag containing 15 blue marbles and 5 green marbles.
- The probability of randomly picking a red marble from a bag containing 15 blue marbles and 5 green marbles.

Probability is the chance that something will happen. The probability of an event is the ratio of the number of favorable outcomes to the number of possible outcomes when all outcomes are equally likely.

Because there is one favorable outcome of two equally likely outcomes, so the probability of winning a coin toss is ½, or 50%.

Both 3 and 6 are multiples of 3, so there are two favorable outcomes out of six equally likely total outcomes. So, the probability of rolling a multiple of 3 on a die is $\frac{2}{6} = \frac{1}{3} = 33.\overline{3}\%$.

There are five green marbles and fifteen blue marbles in a bag. The probability of picking a green marble is the ratio of green marbles to total marbles, or $\frac{5}{20} = \frac{1}{4} = 25\%$.

Because there are no red marbles in the bag, it is not possible to choose a red marble from the bag. Therefore, the probability of choosing a red marble is 0.

Distinguish between theoretical probability and experimental probability.

Theoretical probability is the expected likelihood of an event. Experimental probability is found by conducting trials and comparing the actual occurrence of an event to the number of trials.

For example, the probability of rolling a 2 on a die is 1/6 because there is one favorable outcome, namely rolling a 2, and six equally possible outcomes. So, theoretically, a 2 would appear 100 times if a die is rolled 600 times. Suppose, however, that a die is actually rolled 600 times, and a 2 appears 90 times. The experimental probability is $\frac{90}{600} = \frac{3}{20}$.

If the die is a fair die, the experimental probability should closely approximate or equal the theoretical probability when many trials are conducted.

Determine the probability that the spinner will land on black and predict the number of times the spinner will land on black if the spinner is spun 100 times.

The probabilities of different outcomes on the spinner are not equally likely. Notice that the black section comprises half the circle. So, the spinner will *probably* land in the black section half the time. So, out of 100 spins, the spinner will land in the black section *about* 50 times.

Examine the data collected from 100 coin tosses. Determine the experimental probability of this tossed coin landing on heads (H).

H	H	T	H	T	T	H	T	H	T
T	T	H	T	H	H	T	H	H	T
H	H	T	T	T	T	H	H	T	H
T	H	T	H	H	T	H	H	T	T
H	H	T	H	T	T	H	H	H	T
H	T	T	T	H	H	T	H	T	T
H	T	H	H	T	H	T	T	H	T
H	T	H	H	T	H	T	H	H	T
H	H	T	T	H	T	H	H	T	H
T	T	H	T	H	H	T	T	T	H

Out of 100 trials, 51 coin flips landed on heads, so the experimental probability of getting heads in a coin toss is 51/100. This is very close to the predicted outcome of 50 heads from 100 tosses based on the theoretical probability that a coin will land on heads ($\frac{1}{2}$, or 50%).

The results of 24 rolls of a die are tabulated below. Determine whether or not the results are consistent with the expected results and explain possible reasons for a discrepancy if one exists.

	1	2	3	4	5	6
Number of times rolled	3	4	8	3	2	4

The results of the experiment are not consistent with the expected results. This could be because the die is "loaded" or because enough trials were not performed in the experiment. To determine whether or not the die is loaded, conduct more trials and see if the results are consistent with the expected results based on the experimental probability seen here.

	1	2	3	4	5	6
Number of times rolled	3	4	8	3	2	4
Experimental probability	$\frac{3}{24} = \frac{1}{8}$	$\frac{4}{24} = \frac{1}{6}$	$\frac{8}{24} = \frac{1}{3}$	$\frac{3}{24} = \frac{1}{8}$	$\frac{2}{24} = \frac{1}{12}$	$\frac{4}{24} = \frac{1}{6}$
Theoretical probability	$\frac{1}{6}$	$\frac{1}{6}$	$\frac{1}{6}$	$\frac{1}{6}$	$\frac{1}{6}$	$\frac{1}{6}$
Expected results $\frac{1}{6} \times \frac{24}{1} = \frac{24}{6} = 4$	4	4	4	4	4	4

The results of 24 rolls of a die are tabulated below. Determine the experimental probability from these results and use it to predict the number of times each result will occur if a number cube is rolled 200 times.

	1	2	3	4	5	6
Number of times rolled	3	4	8	3	2	4

The predicted results of 200 rolls based on the experimental probabilities are shown below.

	1	2	3	4	5	6
Number of times rolled	200	200	200	200	200	200
Experimental probability	$\frac{1}{8}$	$\frac{1}{6}$	$\frac{1}{3}$	$\frac{1}{8}$	$\frac{1}{12}$	$\frac{1}{6}$
Predicted results	$\frac{200}{8} = 25$	$\frac{200}{6} \approx 33$	$\frac{200}{3} \approx 67$	$\frac{200}{8} = 25$	$\frac{200}{12} \approx 17$	$\frac{200}{6} \approx 33$

Note that every predicted result is rounded to the nearest whole number since there cannot exist a fraction of a roll. Check to makesure the sum of the rounded numbers is 200: 25+33+67+25+17+33=200.

If the die is indeed loaded, these would be the predicted results. If the die is fair, the results of 200 rolls should show an even distribution of around 33 or 34 rolls over all outcomes.

Joseph is in a math class with 23 other students, 14 of whom are girls. If a student is selected at random from the class, determine the probability that:

- The student selected is Joseph.
- The student selected is a boy.

Since each student has an equally likely chance of being selected from the class, the probability of selecting Joseph is $\dfrac{1}{number\ of\ students\ in\ the\ class}$. The number of students in the class, including Joseph, is 24. So, $P(\text{Joseph}) = \dfrac{1}{24}$.

Since each student has an equally likely chance of being selected from the class, the probability of selecting a boy is $\dfrac{number\ of\ boys\ in\ the\ class}{number\ of\ students\ in\ the\ class}$. Since 14 of the 24 students are girls, there are 10 boys. So, $P(\text{boy}) = \dfrac{10}{24} = \dfrac{5}{12}$.

A baby inherited one copy of a beta-globin gene from her mother and one from her father. Both the baby's mother and father are carriers for sickle cell anemia, meaning that each parent contains a normal allele for beta-globin called type A, and a recessive allele which has a single mutation called type S. The Punnet square below shows the possible genotypes (types of genes) and phenotypes (expressions of the genotypes). Determine the probability that the baby has sickle cell anemia. Express the probabilities as a fraction and as a percent.

	A	S
A	AA (no disease)	AS (no disease/carrier)
S	AS (no disease/carrier)	SS (sickle cell anemia)

The probability that the baby will have sickle cell anemia is ¼, or 25%.

	A	S
A	AA (no disease)	AS (no disease/carrier)
a	AS (no disease/carrier)	SS (sickle cell anemia)

Determine the probability that the baby has inherited a mutated allele from at least one of her parents. Express the probabilities as a fraction and as a percent.

	A	S
A	AA (no disease)	AS (no disease/carrier)
S	AS (no disease/carrier)	SS (sickle cell anemia)

The probability that the baby has inherited a mutated allele from at least one of her parents is ¾, or 75%.

	A	S
A	AA (no disease)	AS (no disease/carrier)
a	AS (no disease/carrier)	SS (sickle cell anemia)

Determine the probability that the baby does not have the disease but carries one copy of the mutated allele. Express the probabilities as a fraction and as a percent.

	A	S
A	AA (no disease)	AS (no disease/carrier)
S	AS (no disease/carrier)	SS (sickle cell anemia)

The probability that the baby does not have the disease but carries one copy of the mutated allele is $\frac{2}{4} = \frac{1}{2}$, or 50%.

	A	S
A	AA (no disease)	AS (no disease/carrier)
a	AS (no disease/carrier)	SS (sickle cell anemia)

Show the sample space for rolling two dice and find the probability of rolling double sixes.

Since there are six outcomes for each die, there are $6 \times 6 = 36$ outcomes for rolling two dice.

1,1	1,2	1,3	1,4	1,5	1,6
2,1	2,2	2,3	2,4	2,5	2,6
3,1	3,2	3,3	3,4	3,5	3,6
4,1	4,2	4,3	4,4	4,5	4,6
5,1	5,2	5,3	5,4	5,5	5,6
6,1	6,2	6,3	6,4	6,5	6,6

For fair dice, each outcome is equally likely. So, the probability can be found $\frac{number\ of\ double\ sixes}{number\ of\ outcomes}$

Only one of the 36 possible outcomes is double sixes, so the probability of getting double sixes is $\frac{1}{36}$.

- 53 -

Use a tree diagram to determine the probability that of two cards pulled from two different decks, at least one is a heart.

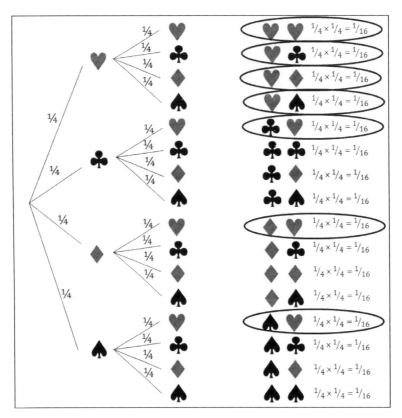

The probability of getting at least one heart includes the outcomes in which a heart is selected from the first deck, in which a heart is selected from the second deck, and in which a heart is selected from both decks. Seven of the sixteen outcomes include at least one heart, so the probability that at least one of the two cards drawn is a heart is $\frac{7}{16}$.

Use a tree diagram to determine the probability that two cards pulled from two different decks are both spades.

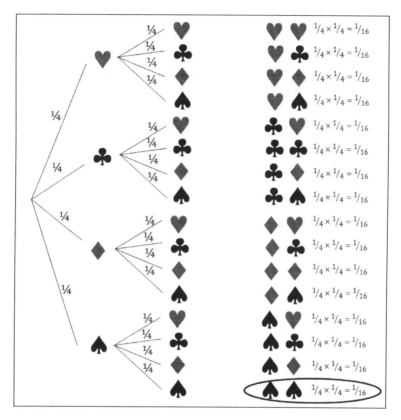

One out of sixteen outcomes is drawing a spade from both decks. So, the probability that both cards are spades is $\frac{1}{16}$.

Notice that the probability of each outcome in the sample space can be found by multiplying the probability of the first event by the probability of the second event.

Suppose a couple has a ¼ chance of having a child with sickle cell anemia. Explain whether or not each statement is true.

- If the couple's first child has sickle cell anemia, then their second child will not have sickle cell anemia.
- If the couple has eight children, two of them will have sickle cell anemia.
- If the couple has six children, it is unlikely that all of them will have sickle cell anemia.

The statement *If the couple's first child has sickle cell anemia, then their second child will not have sickle cell anemia* is **not necessarily true**. If a couple's first child is affected, it is possible for second child to have the disease, too. Each child conceived by the couple has a ¼ chance of developing the disease. The fact that the first child has the disease has no effect on the second child's chance of having it.

The statement *If a couple has eight children, two of them will have sickle cell anemia* is **not necessarily true**. You can <u>predict</u> based on the probability that one in four of the couple's children will be affected that, of eight children, two will have the disease. However, it is possible that none, all, or any number of the children will have the disease.

- 55 -

The statement *If the couple has six children, it is unlikely that all of them will have sickle cell anemia* is **true**. This statement mentions only the relative likelihood of an occurrence. The probability that all six children would have the disease is $\frac{1}{4} \times \frac{1}{4} \times \frac{1}{4} \times \frac{1}{4} \times \frac{1}{4} \times \frac{1}{4} = \frac{1}{4096}$. A probability of $\frac{1}{4096}$ indicates that is unlikely for all six children to have the disease.

Practice Test #1

Practice Questions

1. Ana has completed approximately $\frac{2}{7}$ of her research paper. Which of the following best represents the percentage of the paper she has completed?

    a. 24%
    b. 26%
    c. 27%
    d. 29%

2. Simplify the expression: $2n + (3n - 2)^2$

_____

3. Elijah has prepared $2\frac{1}{2}$ gallons of lemonade to distribute to guests at a party. If there are 25 guests, how much lemonade is available to each guest, given that each guest receives an equal amount?

    a. $\frac{1}{8}$ of a gallon
    b. $\frac{1}{6}$ of a gallon
    c. $\frac{1}{12}$ of a gallon
    d. $\frac{1}{10}$ of a gallon

4. Elijah has prepared $2\frac{1}{2}$ gallons of lemonade to distribute to guests at a party. If there are 25 guests, how much lemonade is available to each guest, given that each guest receives an equal amount?

    a. $\frac{1}{8}$ of a gallon
    b. $\frac{1}{6}$ of a gallon
    c. $\frac{1}{12}$ of a gallon
    d. $\frac{1}{10}$ of a gallon

5. The points M, N, and O are plotted on the number line below. Plot point P based on the equation: $N - M + O = P$. Explain why your answer is correct.

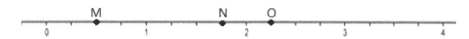

_____

_____

_____

6. Part A: Edward spins the spinner below three times. If the spinner lands on a different number each time what is the highest total he could get?

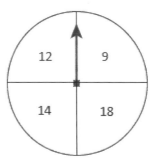

_____

Part B: He decides to spin it one more time. What is the probability that he will land on a number that he has already landed on?

_____

7. A bag of coffee costs $9.85 and contains 16 ounces of coffee. Which of the following best represents the cost per ounce?

 a. $0.67
 b. $0.64
 c. $0.65
 d. $0.62

8. Which of the following is equivalent to $4^3 + 12 \div 4 + 8^2 \times 3$?

 a. 249
 b. 393
 c. 211
 d. 259

9. Part A: The ingredients needed for a cake are given below:

 • 2 eggs
 • $1\frac{3}{4}$ cups of flour
 • 2 teaspoons baking soda
 • ½ cup butter
 • $1\frac{1}{4}$ teaspoons vanilla extract
 • $\frac{3}{4}$ cup of milk

What is the ratio of butter to flour?

 a. 1:3
 b. 2:5
 c. 2:7
 d. 3:2

Part B: When Lucy is making the cake she accidently puts a whole cup of milk in it. What was the ratio of milk to flour before and what is it now?

_____   _____

10. Part A: The original price of a jacket is $36.95. The jacket is discounted by 25%. Before tax, which of the following best represents the cost of the jacket?

    a. $27.34
    b. $27.71
    c. $28.82
    d. $29.56

Part B: If tax is 8% how much does it cost?

_____

11. Martin and his friends are taking a road trip from Houston, TX to Las Vegas, NV. The trip will take two days and they will spend the night in El Paso, TX. The first day they drove for 11 hours at a rate of 69 miles per hour. The next day they drove for 10 hours at a rate of 72 miles per hour. How far is it from Houston to Las Vegas? Explain how you came up with your answer.

_____

_____

_____

12. A bottle of lotion contains 20 fluid ounces and costs $3.96. Which of the following best represents the cost per fluid ounce?

    a. $0.18
    b. $0.20
    c. $0.22
    d. $0.24

13. Solve the equation for x: $3^2 + 2x = 17$.

_____

14. Which of the following graphs accurately portrays the relationship between number of feet and number of yards?

a.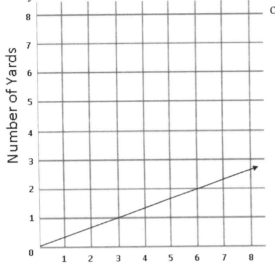
Number of Feet

c.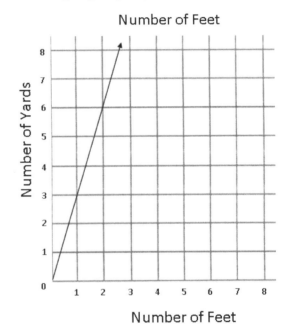
Number of Feet

b.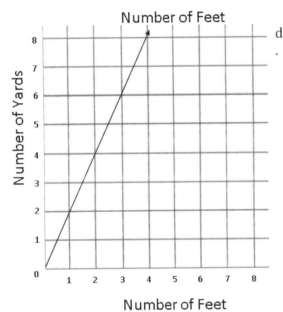
Number of Feet

d.
Number of Feet

15. Given the figure below what is the area of the shaded regions? Figure is not to scale.

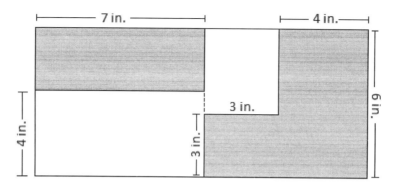

16. Given the sequence represented in the table below, where n represents the position of the term and a_n represents the value of the term, which of the following describes the relationship between the position number and the value of the term? Explain why your answer is correct.

n	1	2	3	4	5	6
a_n	5	2	−1	−4	−7	−10

    a. Multiply n by 2 and subtract 4
    b. Multiply n by 2 and subtract 3
    c. Multiply n by −3 and add 8
    d. Multiply n by −4 and add 1

17. The number 123 is the 11th term in a sequence with a constant rate of change. Which of the following sequences has this number as its 11th term?
    a. 5, 17, 29, 41, …
    b. 3, 15, 27, 39, …
    c. −1, 11, 23, 35, …
    d. 1, 13, 25, 37, …

18. Kevin pays $12.95 for a text messaging service plus $0.07 for each text message he sends. Which of the following equations could be used to represent the total cost, y, when x represents the number of text messages sent?
    a. $y = \$12.95x + \$0.07$
    b. $y = \$13.02x$
    c. $y = \frac{\$12.95}{\$0.07}x$
    d. $y = \$0.07x + \$12.95$

19. Hannah draws two supplementary angles. One angle measures 34°. What is the measure of the other angle?

   a. 56°
   b. 66°
   c. 146°
   d. 326°

20. Part A: Steven's class had a pushup contest and the results are recorded below.

What is the median number of pushups the class did? Explain the process you used to find your answer.

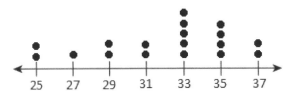

_____

_____

_____

Part B: What is the difference between the median and the mean number of pushups?

_____

21. A triangle has the following angle measures: 98°, 47°, and 35°. What type of triangle is it?

   a. Obtuse
   b. Right
   c. Acute
   d. Equiangular

22. Part A: Jordan has a bag full of red and blue marbles. There are 16 red marbles and 24 blue marbles? What is the probability of him drawing a red marble?

_____

Part B: Jordan has continued to draw marbles and has now taken out 4 red and 6 blue. What is the probability of him drawing a red marble now?

_____

23. Which figure has two circular bases and a lateral face?

   a. Cone
   b. Prism
   c. Cylinder
   d. Sphere

24. Edward draws a triangle with vertices at (1, 4), (5, 1), and (5, 6). If he wishes to reflect the triangle across the x-axis, which of the following vertices should he plot?

    a. (−1, 4), (−5, 1), (−5, 6)
    b. (1, −4), (5, −1), (5, −6)
    c. (−1, −4), (−5, −1), (−5, −6)
    d. (4, 1), (1, 5), (6, 5)

25. Plot the two ordered pairs on the graph below: (x-3, 5) and (7-x, -2) where x = 2.

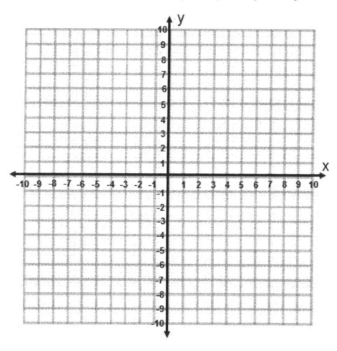

26. Bookstore A sells a particular book for $15.25, but they have it on sale for 20% off. Bookstore B sells it for $12.45. How much more does it cost at Bookstore B?

_____

27. A carpenter must fix a broken section of a kitchen cabinet. The intact portion of the cabinet forms a 76 degree angle with the wall. The width of the cabinet is supposed to form a 90 degree angle with the wall. What angle measure should the carpenter use when cutting the piece that will fit next to the 76 degree angle?

    a. 12°
    b. 14°
    c. 104°
    d. 136°

- 63 -

28. Which of the following represents the net of a triangular prism?

a.

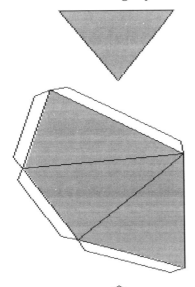

c.

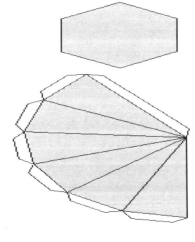

b.

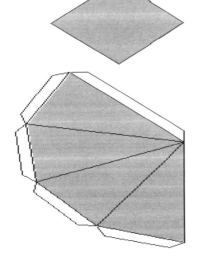

d.

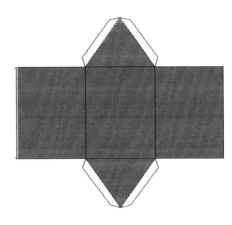

29. A circle has a radius of 23 cm. Which of the following is the best estimate for the circumference of the circle?

    a. 71.76 cm
    b. 143.52 cm
    c. 144.44 cm
    d. 72.22 cm

30. Sally is driving to the store. It takes her $\frac{1}{12}$ of an hour to go 3.4 miles. How many miles an hour is Sally driving?

    a. 36 mph
    b. 17 mph
    c. 40.8 mph
    d. 42.4 mph

31. Which of the following is also equal to $4n^2 + (3n + 5)^2$? Select all that apply.
1. $2n^2 + 2n^2 + (3n + 5)^2$
2. $4n^2 + (3n^2 + 25)$
3. $4n^2 + (3n + 5)$
4. $13n^2 + 30n + 25$
5. $7n^2 + 25$

32. Ashton draws the parallelogram shown below. How many square units represent the area of the parallelogram?

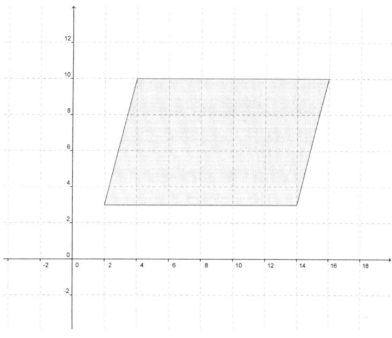

33. In the formula for the volume of the figure shown below, written as $V = B \cdot h$, h represents the height of the prism when it rests one of its bases. What does the B represent?

h

a. $\frac{1}{3}bh$, where b represents the length of the triangle's base and h represents the triangle's height

b. bh, where b represents the length of the triangle's base and h represents the triangle's height

c. $2bh$, where b represents the length of triangle's base and h represents the triangle's height

d. $\frac{1}{2}bh$, where b represents the length of triangle's base and h represents the triangle's height

34. A rectangular prism has a length of 14.3 cm, a width of 8.9 cm, and a height of 11.7 cm. Which of the following is the best estimate for the volume of the rectangular prism?

    a. 1,512 cm^3
    b. 1,287 cm^3
    c. 1,386 cm^3
    d. 1,620 cm^3

35. A can has a radius of 3.5 cm and a height of 8 cm. Which of the following best represents the volume of the can?

    a. 294.86 cm^3
    b. 298.48 cm^3
    c. 307.72 cm^3
    d. 309.24 cm^3

36. Fred designs a candy box in the shape of a triangular prism. The base of each triangular face measures 4 inches, while the height of the prism is 7 inches. Given that the length of the prism is 11 inches, what is the volume of the candy box?

    a. 102 in^3
    b. 128 in^3
    c. 154 in^3
    d. 308 in^3

37. Miranda rolls a standard die and spins a spinner with 4 equal sections. Which of the following represents the sample space?

    a. 10
    b. 12
    c. 24
    d. 36

38. A hat contains 6 red die, 4 green die, and 2 blue die. What is the probability that Sarah pulls out a blue die, replaces it, and then pulls out a green die? Explain why your answer is correct.

    a. $\frac{1}{18}$
    b. $\frac{1}{3}$
    c. $\frac{1}{2}$
    d. $\frac{1}{16}$

_____

_____

_____

39. Which figure has 5 faces and 8 edges?

    a. Triangular pyramid
    b. Cube
    c. Square pyramid
    d. Triangular prism

40. The histogram below represents the overall GRE scores for a sample of college students. Which of the following is a true statement?

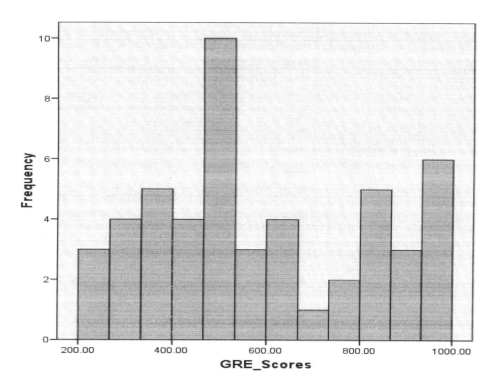

a. The range of GRE scores is approximately 600
b. The average GRE score is 750
c. The median GRE score is approximately 500
d. The fewest number of college students had an approximate score of 800

- 67 -

41. What is the area of the circle on the graph below? Each square represents 1 inch.

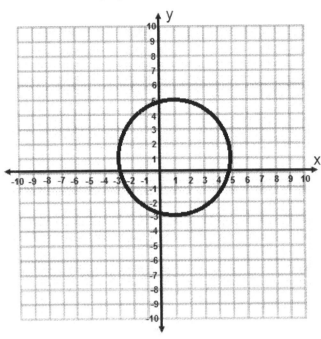

---

42. Raymond has the triangular prism shown below. If he cuts two-dimensional slices out of it how many different shapes could he make?

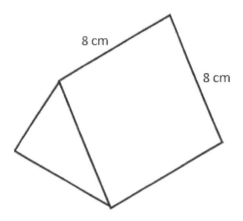

a. 2, a triangle and a rectangle
b. 1, a triangle
c. 2, a square and a rectangle
d. 3, a square, a triangle, and a rectangle

43. Gabriel went to a taco shop for lunch. He ordered 3 tacos and paid $4.14. The next day he decided to try a different taco shop and ordered 4 tacos and paid $4.80. How much more expensive was the first taco shop per taco? Express your answer as a percent.

---

44. Amy rolled a die and flipped a coin and spun a spinner with four equal sections numbered 1-4. What is the probability that she rolled an even number, got heads and then spun an even number?

  a. $\dfrac{1}{4}$

  b. $\dfrac{1}{2}$

  c. $\dfrac{3}{4}$

  d. $\dfrac{1}{8}$

45. Seth and Haden were arguing one day about which one had a bigger room. Seth's argument was that his was bigger because it was 12 feet by 13 feet while Haden's is 10 by 14 feet. So, his argument is that he has more square footage. Haden's argument was that his was bigger because his ceiling was 9 feet tall while Seth's is only 8 feet tall. He was arguing that he had more cubic feet. Which of the following choices best explains who is right?

  a. Only Seth is right.
  b. Only Haden is right
  c. Neither one of them is right.
  d. They are each right.

46. The ages at which a sample of female dogs is spayed is shown below. Based on this sample, what is the average age a female dog gets spayed? 6, 7, 2, 8, 4, 1, 7, 8, 3, 1, 8, 2

  a. 3.75
  b. 4
  c. 4.75
  d. 5

Answers and Explanations

1. D: In order to convert the given fraction to a percentage, divide 2 by 7. Doing so gives a decimal of approximately 0.29. The decimal can be converted to a percentage by multiplying by 100, which moves the decimal point two places to the right and gives 29%.

2. $2n + (3n - 2)^2 = 2n + 9n^2 - 6n - 6n + 4 = 9n^2 - 10n + 4$

3. D: In order to determine the amount available to each guest, the total amount of prepared lemonade should be divided by 25 guests. Thus, the expression $2\frac{1}{2} \div 25$ represents the amount that each guest has available for consumption. The mixed fraction can be rewritten as $\frac{5}{2}$. The expression can be simplified by writing $\frac{5}{2} \div 25 = \frac{5}{2} \times \frac{1}{25}$, which equals $\frac{5}{50}$, or $\frac{1}{10}$.

4. D: In order to determine the amount available to each guest, the total amount of prepared lemonade should be divided by 25 guests. Thus, the expression $2\frac{1}{2} \div 25$ represents the amount that each guest has available for consumption. The mixed fraction can be rewritten as $\frac{5}{2}$. The expression can be simplified by writing $\frac{5}{2} \div 25 = \frac{5}{2} \times \frac{1}{25}$, which equals $\frac{5}{50}$, or $\frac{1}{10}$.

5. M=$\frac{1}{2}$, N=$1\frac{3}{4}$, and O=$2\frac{1}{4}$, so N-M+O=$3\frac{1}{2}$. The number line is shown below.

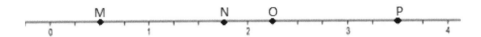

6. Part A: 44: I the spinner must land on a different number each time then the highest three numbers are 12,14, and 18. Added together they equal 44.

Part B: $\frac{3}{4}$: He has already landed on three of the four numbers so the probability is $\frac{3}{4}$.

7. D: The cost per ounce can be calculated by dividing the cost of the bag by the number of ounces the bag contains. Thus, the cost per ounce can be calculated by writing $9.85 ÷ 16, which equals approximately $0.62 per ounce.

8. D: The order of operations states that numbers with exponents must be evaluated first. Thus, the expression can be rewritten as $64 + 12 \div 4 + 64 \times 3$. Next, multiplication and division must be computed as they appear from left to right in the expression. Thus, the expression can be further simplified as $64 + 3 + 192$, which equals 259.

9. Part A: C: Both flour and butter are given in cups so they are easy to compare. First find a like denominator. $\frac{1}{2}$ is equal to $\frac{2}{4}$, and $1\frac{3}{4}$ is equal to $\frac{7}{4}$. So the ratio is 2:7.

Part B: 3:7, 4:7: This question is very similar to Part A. Both milk and flour are given in cups and fourths. It's $\frac{3}{4}$ to $\frac{7}{4}$ or 3:7, and if she puts a whole cup in then its $\frac{4}{4}$ to $\frac{7}{4}$ or 4:7.

10. Part A: B: The discounted price is 25% less than the original price. Therefore, the discounted price can be written as $36.95 - ((0.25)(36.95))$, which equals approximately 27.71. Thus, the discounted price of the jacket is $27.71.

Part B: $29.93: If sales tax is 8% then that can be written as ($27.71)(1.08), which is approximately $29.93.

11. 1479 miles: The first day they went 69 miles per hour for 11 hours, so they went $11 \times 69 = 759 \; miles$. The second day they went 72 miles per hour for 10 hours, so they went $10 \times 72 = 720 \; miles$. Total they went 1479 miles.

12. B: In order to find the unit rate, the cost of the bottle should be divided by the number of fluid ounces contained in the bottle: $\frac{\$3.96}{20} \approx 0.20$. Thus, the cost per fluid ounce is approximately $0.20.

13. X=4: $3^2 + 2x = 17, 9 + 2x = 17, 2x = 8, x = 4$

14. A: The graph shown for Choice A is the line $y = \frac{1}{3}x$, where both measurable quantities x and y are greater than or equal to zero Since 1 foot is one-third of a yard, this equation is representative of the relationship between number of feet and number of yards.

15. 45 square inches: The top left shaded region can be found by first finding the width. Since 6 in. is given as the width of the whole rectangle and 4 in. is given for the width of the non shaded region then the width of the shaded region is the difference of 2 inches. So, the area of that region is $7 \; in. \times 2 in. = 14 \; square \; inches$. The other shaded region can be broken into a 3 in. by 3 in. square and a 4 in. by 6 in. rectangle. So, $3 \; in. \times 3 \; in. = 9 \; ssquare \; inches$ and $4 \; in. \times 6 \; in. = 24 \; square \; inches$. Added together the total area is 45 square inches.

16. C: The equation that represents the relationship between the position number, n, and the value of the term, a_n, is $a_n = -3n + 8$. Notice each n is multiplied by –3, with 8 added to that value. Substituting position number 1 for n gives $a_n = -3(1) + 8$, which equals 5. Substitution of the remaining position numbers does not provide a counterexample to this procedure.

17. B: All given sequences have a constant difference of 12. Subtraction of 12 from the starting term, given for Choice B, gives a y-intercept of –9. The equation $123 = 12x - 9$ can thus be written. Solving for x gives $x = 11$; therefore, 123 is indeed the 11th term of this sequence. Manual computation of the 11th term by adding the constant difference of 12 also reveals 123 as the value of the 11th term of this sequence.

18. D: The constant amount Kevin pays is $12.95; this amount represents the y-intercept. The variable amount is represented by the expression $0.07x$, where x represents the number of text messages sent and $0.07 represents the constant rate of change or slope. Thus, his total cost can be represented by the equation $y = \$0.07x + \$12.95$.

19. C: Supplementary angles add to 180 degrees. Therefore, the other angle is equal to the difference between 180 degrees and 34 degrees: $180 - 34 = 146$. Thus, the other angle measures 146°.

20. Part A: 33: The median number is the middle number out of the group. In this case there are 18 numbers so it is the average of the 9th and 10th number. However, since the 9th and 10th numbers are both 33 it is just 33.

Part B: 1: The mean can be found by adding all of the numbers together and dividing by 18. If you add all of the numbers up and divide by 18 you get 32. The difference in the mean and median is 1.

21. A: A triangle with an obtuse angle (an angle greater than 90°) is called an obtuse triangle.

22. Part A: $\frac{2}{5}$: There are a total of 40 marbles in the bag. The probability of him drawing a red one is $\frac{16}{40}$ or $\frac{2}{5}$.

Part B: $\frac{2}{3}$: If 4 red and 6 blue are missing then there are only 12 red and 18 blue remaining. The probability of drawing a red one then is $\frac{12}{18}$ or $\frac{2}{3}$.

23. C: A cylinder has two circular bases and a rectangular lateral face.

24. B: A reflection of a figure across the x-axis involves finding the negation (or additive inverse) of the y-value of each coordinate; the x-value stays the same. Negating each y-value gives the vertices (1, −4), (5, −1), and (5, −6).

25. The point (x-3, 5) is (2-3, 5) or (-1, 5). The point (7-x, -2) is (7-2, -2) or (5, -2). Both are graphed below.

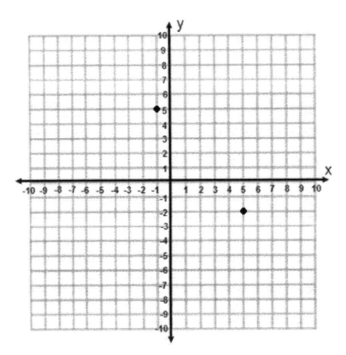

26. $.25: First find the cost of the book at Bookstore A. The price would be $15.25(.8) = $12.20. The cost at Bookstore B is $12.45 so it is $.25 more.

27. B: Since the intact portion of the cabinet and the missing piece form a 90 degree angle with the wall, the missing piece must have an angle equal to the difference between 90 degrees and 76 degrees. Thus, the newly cut cabinet piece should have an angle measure of 14 degrees.

28. D: A triangular prism has two triangular bases and three rectangular faces.

29. C: The circumference of a circle can be determined by using the formula $C = \pi d$. A radius of 23 cm indicates a diameter of 46 cm, or twice that length. Substitution of 46 cm for d and 3.14 for π gives the following: $C = 3.14 \cdot 46$, which equals 144.44. Thus, the circumference of the circle is approximately 144.44 cm.

30. C: If she goes 3.4 miles in $\frac{1}{12}$ of an hour then just multiply by 12 to see how far she will go in one hour. Then that is her miles per hour.

31. I, IV: Start by simplifying the equation. $4n^2 + (3n + 5)^2 = 4n^2 + 9n^2 + 15n + 15n + 25 = 13n^2 + 30n + 25$. So, you can see that you came up with answer IV right there, and answer I is the same as the original equation except for the $4n^2$ is broken down to $2n^2 + 2n^2$.

32. 84: The area of a parallelogram can be found by using the formula $A = bh$, where b represents the length of the base and h represents the height of the parallelogram. The base and the height of the parallelogram are 12 units and 7 units, respectively. Therefore, the area can be written as $A = 12 \cdot 7$, which equals 84.

33. D: The B in the formula $V = Bh$ represents the area of the triangular base. The formula for the area of a triangle is $\frac{1}{2}bh$, where b represents the length of the triangle's base and h represents the triangle's height.

34. A: The dimensions of the rectangular prism can be rounded to 14 cm, 9 cm, and 12 cm. The volume of a rectangular prism can be determined by finding the product of the length, width, and height. Therefore, the volume is approximately equal to $14 \times 9 \times 12$, or $1{,}512$ cm^3.

35. C: The volume of a cylindrical can be found using the formula $V = \pi r^2 h$, where r represents the radius and h represents the height. Substitution of the given radius and height gives $V = \pi(3.5)^2 \cdot 8$, which is approximately 307.72. Thus, the volume of the can is approximately 307.72 cm^3.

36. C: The volume of a triangular prism can be determined using the formula $V = \frac{1}{2}bhl$, where b represents the length of the base of each triangular face, h represents the height of each triangular face, and l represents the length of the prism. Substitution of the given values into the formula gives $V = \frac{1}{2} \cdot 4 \cdot 7 \cdot 11$, which equals 154. Thus, the volume of the candy box is 154 cubic inches.

37. C: The sample space of independent events is equal to the product of the sample space of each event. The sample space of rolling a die is 6; the sample space of spinning a spinner with four equal sections is 4. Therefore, the overall sample space is equal to 6×4, or 24.

38. A: The events are independent since Sarah replaces the first die. The probability of two independent events can be found using the formula $P(A \text{ and } B) = P(A) \cdot P(B)$. The probability of pulling out a blue die is $\frac{2}{12}$. The probability of pulling out a green die is $\frac{4}{12}$. The probability of pulling out a blue die and a green die is $\frac{2}{12} \cdot \frac{4}{12}$, which simplifies to $\frac{1}{18}$.

39. C: A square pyramid has 5 faces and 8 edges. There are four triangular faces and a square base.

40. C: The score that has approximately 50% above and 50% below is approximately 500 (517 to be exact). The scores can be manually written by choosing either the lower or upper end of each interval and using the frequency to determine the number of times to record each score, i.e., using the lower end of each interval shows an approximate value of 465 for the median; using the upper end of each interval shows an approximate value of 530 for the median. A score of 500 (and the exact median of 517) is found between 465 and 530.

41. 16π or 50.27 inches: The area of a circle is πr^2. You can find the radius by counting the number of units across the circle and dividing by 2. So the radius is 4 inches. $\pi 4^2 = 16\pi$ or 50.27 *inches*.

42. D: If you were to cut a slice vertically it would produce a triangle. If you were to cut a slice long ways it would produce a rectangle, and if you were to cut a slice that was the front face of the prism it would be an 8 by 8 square.

43. 15%: First find the cost of the first taco shop by dividing $4.14 by 3, which comes out to $1.38 per taco. Then find the price at the second shop by dividing $4.80 by 4 to get $1.20 per taco. The difference is .$18. To get a percentage divide $.18 by $1.20 and multiply by 100. The first shop cost 15% more than the second.

44. D: The probability of getting an even number is $\frac{3}{6}$. The probability of getting heads is $\frac{1}{2}$. The probability of spinning an even number is $\frac{2}{4}$. The probability of all three occurring can be calculated by multiplying the probabilities of the individual events: $\frac{3}{6} \cdot \frac{1}{2} \cdot \frac{2}{4}$ equals $\frac{1}{8}$.

45. D: They are both right in their own respect. Seth's room has 156 sq. feet while Haden's only has 140 sq. feet. However, because Haden has a 9 foot ceiling he has 1260 cubic feet compared to Seth's 1248 cubic feet.

46. C: The average age indicates the mean. The mean is calculated by summing all ages and dividing by the number of dogs in the sample. Thus, the mean can be calculated by writing $\frac{6+7+2+8+4+1+7+8+3+1+8+2}{12}$, which equals 4.75.

Practice Test #2

Practice Questions

1. Which of the following is the largest number? Explain why your answer is correct.

$$\frac{14}{4}, 3.41, \pi, 3\frac{3}{8}$$

[handwritten: 14/4, 3.41, 3⅜, π.]

_____

_____

_____

2. A plane takes off from Dallas and lands in New York 3 hours and 20 minutes later. The distance from Dallas to New York is 1510 miles. Approximately how fast was the plane traveling?

   a. 445 mph
   b. 453 mph
   c. 456 mph
   d. 449 mph

3. According to the order of operations, which of the following steps should be completed immediately following the evaluation of the squared number when evaluating the expression $9 - 18^2 \times 2 + 12 \div 4$?

   a. Subtract 18^2 from 9
   b. Multiply the squared value by 2
   c. Divide 12 by 4
   d. Add 2 and 12

4. A parcel of land has 35 mature trees for every 3 acres. How many mature trees can be found on 18 of the acres?

   a. 206
   b. 212
   c. 210
   d. 214

5. Which of the following is equivalent to $-8^2 + (17 - 9) \times 4 + 7$?

   a. -217
   b. 24
   c. -64
   d. -25

6. Jason chooses a number that is the square root of four less than two times Amy's number. If Amy's number is 20, what is Jason's number?

   a. 6
   b. 7
   c. 8
   d. 9

7. The 12ᵗʰ term in a sequence with a common difference of −9 is −106. Which of the following formulas can be used to represent this sequence?

    a. $y = -9x + 4$
    b. $y = -9x - 6$
    c. $y = -9x + 2$
    d. $y = -9x - 8$

8. Which of the following statements is true?

    a. All rectangles are squares
    b. All rhombi are squares
    c. All squares are rhombi
    d. All parallelograms are rectangles

9. Part A: What is the area of the shaded region below?

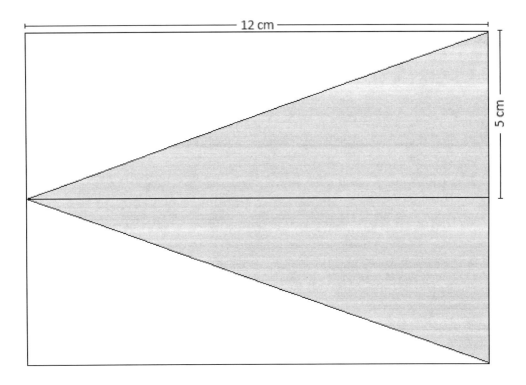

Part B: How does the shaded region compare to the non shaded region?

    a. The shaded region is bigger than the non shaded region
    b. Both the shaded and non shaded region are the same size
    c. The non shaded region is bigger than the shaded region
    d. The area of the non shaded region cannot be determined

10. Given the table below what would y be if $x=5$?

X	-2	0	3	4
y	2	-2	7	14

    a. 21
    b. 23
    c. 19
    d. 24

11. Given the following equation what is x equal to if y equals 8? $6x + 4 = 2y - 7$.

_____

12. A landscaping company charges \$25 per $\frac{1}{2}$-acre to mow a yard. The company is offering a 20% discount for the month of May. If Douglas has a two-acre yard, how much will the company charge?
    a. \$65
    b. \$80
    c. \$70
    d. \$75

13. A house is priced at \$278,000. The price of the house has been reduced by \$12,600. Which of the following best represents the percentage of the reduction?
    a. 3%
    b. 4%
    c. 5%
    d. 6%

14. Amy buys 4 apples and 3 bananas at the grocery store. She spent a total of \$5.17. Each apple cost \$.94. If each banana cost the same amount how much did one banana cost? Explain why your answer is correct.

_____

_____

_____

15. Melanie makes \$12 an hour and is taxed at 15% on her income. Lynn makes \$14 an hour and is taxed at 18% on her income. If they both work a 40 hour week, how much more does Lynn make than Melanie?

_____

16. A cone has a radius of 4 cm and an approximate volume of 150.72 cm^3. What is the height of the cone?
    a. 7 cm
    b. 9 cm
    c. 8 cm
    d. 12 cm

17. What is the range of the points on the number line below?

_____

18. Complete the equation below.

$2\frac{5}{8} - \frac{3}{2} + \left(\frac{2}{3} - \frac{1}{6}\right) = 1\frac{1}{8} +$ _____ = _____

19. Point S and Point T are shown on the number line below. Which of the following equations produces a point, R, not on the number line? Explain why your answer is correct.

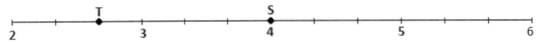

   a. 2S-T=R
   b. 2T-S=R
   c. 3T-S=R
   d. 3S-2T=R

_____

_____

_____

20. Part A: The spinner below is spun once. What is the probability of landing on a 12 or greater?

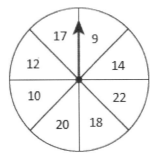

   a. $\frac{5}{8}$
   b. $\frac{1}{2}$
   c. $\frac{3}{4}$
   d. $\frac{2}{8}$

Part B: What is the probability of spinning it a second time and getting a 12 or greater both times?

_____

21. A toy store owner sells action figures. He buys each one from the manufacture for $4.10. He has labor and other costs of $1.35 per action figure. He wants to make a 32% profit on each one. How much does he need to sell them for?

_____

_____

_____

22. Angle A and Angle B are complementary. Angle B measures 28°. What is the measure of Angle A?

   a. 62°
   b. 92°
   c. 72°
   d. 152°

23. Which of the following describes *all* requirements of similar polygons?

   a. Similar polygons have congruent corresponding angles and proportional corresponding sides
   b. Similar polygons have congruent corresponding angles and congruent corresponding sides
   c. Similar polygons have proportional corresponding sides
   d. Similar polygons have congruent corresponding angles

24. How far apart are the two points on the graph below? Each square represents 3 feet.

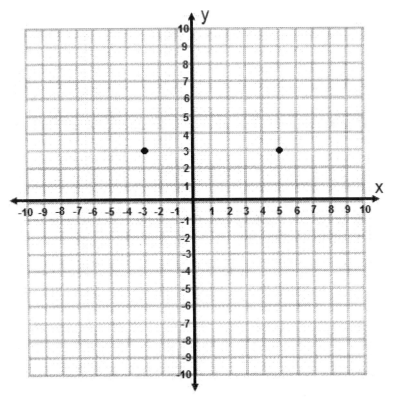

    a. 15 feet
    b. 22 feet
    c. 21 feet
    d. 24 feet

25. Eric is able to dribble the soccer ball down $\frac{2}{3}$ of the field in $\frac{2}{5}$ of a minute. How long will it take him to dribble the whole field?

    a. 36 seconds
    b. 24 seconds
    c. 30 seconds
    d. 32 seconds

26. Kaleb has a bike rim that is 18 inches in diameter. He puts a tire on it that is 2 inches thick. What is the circumference of the tire?

    a. 20π
    b. 22π
    c. 24π
    d. 18π

27. Given the trapezoid shown below, which of the following vertices represent the reflection of the trapezoid across the *y*-axis?

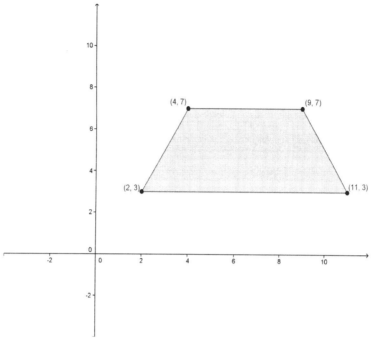

a. (−4, −7), (−9, −7), (−2, −3), (−11, −3)
b. (−4, 7), (−9, 7), (−2, 3), (−11, 3)
c. (7, −4), (7, −9), (3, −2), (3, −11)
d. (4, −7), (9, −7), (2, −3), (11, −3)

28. A regular heptagon has each side length equal to 9.2 cm. Which of the following is the best estimate for the perimeter of the heptagon?

a. 60 cm
b. 63 cm
c. 54 cm
d. 70 cm

29. A parallelogram has two bases, each equal to 18 cm, and a height of 8 cm. What is the area of the parallelogram?

a. 288 cm^2
b. 72 cm^2
c. 144 cm^2
d. 96 cm^2

- 81 -

30. Which of the following represents the area of the triangle shown below?

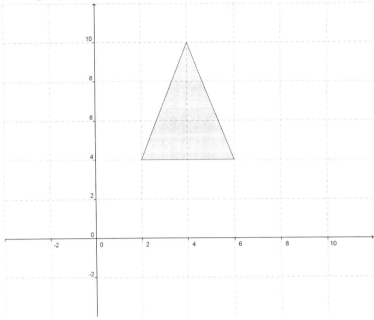

    a. 8 square units
    b. 9 square units
    c. 10 square units
    d. 12 square units

31. Judith purchased a box from the U.S. Postal Service with dimensions of 12 inches by 8 inches by 6 inches. How many cubic inches of space inside the box does she have available for use?

_____

32. A pothole has a radius of 9 inches. Which of the following best represents the distance around the pothole?
    a. 14.13 inches
    b. 28.26 inches
    c. 42.39 inches
    d. 56.52 inches

33. What is the area of a trapezoid with base lengths of 7 cm and 10 cm and a height of 5 cm?
    a. 85 cm^2
    b. 42.5 cm^2
    c. 28 cm^2
    d. 8.5 cm^2

34. What is the sample space when rolling two standard dice?
    a. 18
    b. 6
    c. 12
    d. 36

35. What is the sample space when flipping a coin 9 times? Explain why your answer is correct.

    a. 256

    b. 4,096

    c. 512

    d. 1,028

_____

_____

_____

36. Kevin spins a spinner with 8 sections labeled 1 through 8. He also flips a coin. What is the probability he will land on a number less than 5 and get tails?

    a. $\dfrac{7}{8}$

    b. $\dfrac{1}{4}$

    c. $\dfrac{5}{16}$

    d. $\dfrac{1}{2}$

37. Which of the following formulas represents the value of the nth term as 4 less than 6 times the position of the nth term?

    a. $a_n = 4n - 6$

    b. $a_n = 6n + 4$

    c. $a_n = 6n - 4$

    d. $a_n = n - 10$

38. Marlo needs to build a right triangular brace with an area greater than 49 square inches but less than 52 square inches. Which dimensions should she use for the base and height of the brace?

    a. 6 inches and 18 inches

    b. 13 inches and 8 inches

    c. 11 inches and 9 inches

    d. 7 inches and 14 inches

39. A box contains 8 yellow marbles, 9 orange marbles, and 1 green marble. What is the probability that Ann pulls out a yellow marble, replaces it, and then pulls a green marble?

    a. $\dfrac{4}{153}$

    b. $\dfrac{1}{2}$

    c. $\dfrac{4}{9}$

    d. $\dfrac{2}{81}$

40. The number of flights a flight attendant made per month is represented by the line graph below.

What is the range in the number of flights the flight attendant made?

    a. 20
    b. 25
    c. 29
    d. 32

41. Which figure has four triangular faces and a square base?

    a. Triangular prism
    b. Square prism
    c. Triangular pyramid
    d. Square pyramid

42. Aubrey planted fruit trees on her farm. The number of each type of tree planted is shown in the table below.

Type of Tree	Number of Trees
Apple Tree	8
Peach Tree	18
Fig Tree	12
Pear Tree	3

Which circle graph represents the percentage of each type of tree planted?

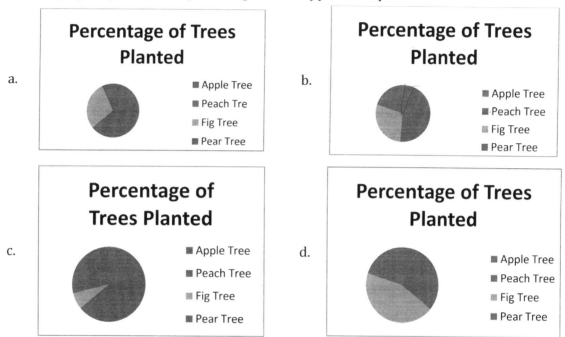

a.

Percentage of Trees Planted
- Apple Tree
- Peach Tre
- Fig Tree
- Pear Tree

b.

Percentage of Trees Planted
- Apple Tree
- Peach Tree
- Fig Tree
- Pear Tree

c.

Percentage of Trees Planted
- Apple Tree
- Peach Tree
- Fig Tree
- Pear Tree

d.

Percentage of Trees Planted
- Apple Tree
- Peach Tree
- Fig Tree
- Pear Tree

43. Chandler wishes to examine the median house value in his new hometown. Which graphical representation will most clearly indicate the median?

    a. Box-and-whisker plot
    b. Stem-and-leaf plot
    c. Line plot
    d. Bar graph

44. Part A: The number of long distance minutes Amanda used per week for business purposes is shown in the table below.

Week	Number of Minutes
1	289
2	255
3	322
4	291
5	306
6	302
7	411
8	418

What is the median number of long distance minutes she used?

_____

Part B: How much more is the mean than the median?

_____

45. A university reported the number of incoming freshmen from 2002 to 2011. The data is shown in the table below.

Year	Number of Incoming Freshmen
2002	7,046
2003	7,412
2004	6,938
2005	7,017
2006	7,692
2007	8,784
2008	7,929
2009	7,086
2010	8,017
2011	8,225

Based on the 10-year sample of data, which of the following represents the approximate average number of incoming freshmen?

    a. 7,618
    b. 7,615
    c. 7,621
    d. 7,624

46. Tina and Josie each walk to school in the morning and then walk home in the afternoon. Tina walks a total of 2.2 miles and it takes her 36 minutes. Josie walks 1.9 miles total and it takes her 30 minutes. Which one of them walks at a faster pace? Explain why your answer is correct.

    a. Tina, she walks at 3.67 miles per hour while Josie only walks at 3.6 miles per hour
    b. Josie, she walks at 3.8 miles per hour while Tina only walks at 3.67 miles per hour
    c. Josie, she walks at 3.6 miles per hour while Tina only walks at 3.5 miles per hour
    d. Tina, she walks at 3.75 miles per hour while Josie only walks at 3.5 miles per hour

_____

_____

_____

Answers and Explanations

1. $\frac{14}{4}$: First you will want to convert all of the numbers to a decimal so they will be easier to compare. $\frac{14}{4} = 3.5$, 3.41, $\pi = 3.14$, $3\frac{3}{8} = 3.375$. Once they are all in decimal form you can see that 3.5 or $\frac{14}{4}$ is the biggest.

2. B: To find miles per hour just divide the number of miles by the number of hours. In this case 3 hours and 20 minutes is equal to $3\frac{1}{3}$ hours. 1510 divided by $3\frac{1}{3}$ is approximately 453 mph.

3. B: The order of operations states that multiplication and division, as they appear from left to right in the expression, should be completed following the evaluation of exponents. Therefore, after evaluating the squared number, that value should be multiplied by 2.

4. C: The following proportion can be used to solve the problem: $\frac{35}{3} = \frac{x}{18}$, where x represents the number of mature trees. Solving for x gives $3x = 630$, which simplifies to $x = 210$.

5. D: The order of operations requires evaluation of the expression inside the parentheses as a first step. Thus, the expression can be re-written as $-8^2 + 8 \times 4 + 7$. Next, the integer with the exponent must be evaluated. Doing so gives $-64 + 8 \times 4 + 7$. The order of operations next requires all multiplications and divisions to be computed as they appear from left to right. Thus, the expression can be written as $-64 + 32 + 7$. Finally, the addition may be computed as it appears from left to right. The expression simplifies to $-32 + 7$, or -25.

6. A: Jason's number can be determined by writing the following expression: $\sqrt{2x - 4}$, where x represents Amy's number. Substitution of 20 for x gives $\sqrt{2(20) - 4}$, which simplifies to $\sqrt{36}$, or 6. Thus, Jason's number is 6. Jason's number can also be determined by working backwards. If Jason's number is the square root of 4 less than 2 times Amy's number, Amy's number should first be multiplied by 2 with 4 subtracted from that product and the square root taken of the resulting difference.

7. C: Evaluation of the formula $y = -9x + 2$ for an x-value of 12 gives a y-value of -106, the value of the 12th term. Thus, the formula given for Choice C can be used to represent the sequence.

8. C: All squares are indeed rhombi because a rhombus is simply a quadrilateral with four equal side lengths. A square is also a quadrilateral with four equal side lengths. Those side lengths simply happen to form right angles.

9. Part A: Since the line that divides the shaded and non shaded region runs from corner to corner it cuts the rectangle in half. This means you can just find the area of the rectangle and divide by 2. However there are two smaller rectangles like this. So, if you take half of each that is the same as one whole rectangle. The area of the rectangle is 5 cm times 12 cm which is 60 cm. Since you would divide by 2 to get the area of one but then multiply back by 2 to get the area of both there is no need to do either. The area of the shaded region is 60 sq cm.

Part B: B: As mentioned in Part A, since the line that divides them cuts the rectangle in half they are the same size.

10. 23: First find the relationship between x and y. When $x=0$ then $y=-2$, so this means that the equation is will have a -2 in it. If you add 2 back to all of the y numbers then you can see that they are the squares of the x's. So the relationship is $y = x^2 - 2$. Then you can just plug in to find the when $x=5, y=23$.

11. $\frac{5}{6}$: First plug 8 in for y to get $6x + 4 = 2(8) - 7$. Then solve for x. $6x + 4 = 16 - 7, 6x = 5, x = \frac{5}{6}$.

12. B: Based on the company's charge per half of an acre, the original charge is equal to 25×4, or $100, since there are 4 half-acres in 2 acres. With the discount of 20%, the following expression can be used to determine the final charge: $x - 0.20x$, where x represents the original charge. Substitution of 100 for x gives $100 - 0.20(100)$, which equals $100 - 20$, or 80. Thus, the company will charge $80.

13. B: The original price was $290,600 ($278,000 + $12,600). In order to determine the percentage of reduction, the following equation can be written: $\$12,600 = \$290,600x$, which simplifies to $x \approx 0.04$, or 4%. Thus, the percentage of reduction was approximately 4%.

14. $.47: The total was $5.17 and the 4 apples cost $3.76. So, $5.17-$3.76=$1.41 that was spent on bananas. Since there were 3 bananas, divide $1.41 by 3 to get $.47 per banana.

15. $51.20: First find what Melanie makes in a week. She makes $12 an hour times 40 hours, so she makes $480. Then take off 15% percent for her taxes. $480(.85)=$408. Next find what Lynn makes in one week. She makes $14 an hour times 40 hours, so she makes $560. Then take 18% off for her taxes. $560(.82)=$459.20. Then subtract what Melanie makes from what Lynn makes to find out how much more Lynn makes. $459.20-$408= $51.20.

16. B: The volume of a cone can be determined by using the formula $V = \frac{1}{3}\pi r^2 h$. Substitution of the radius and volume into the formula gives $150.72 = \frac{1}{3}\pi(4)^2 h$, which simplifies to $150.72 = \frac{1}{3}\pi 16h$. Division of each side of the equation by $\frac{1}{3}\pi 16$ gives $h = 9$. Thus, the height of the cone is 9 cm.

17. 3: The range of the numbers is the difference between the largest and smallest numbers in a set of numbers. In this case each tick mark on the number line represents $\frac{1}{2}$. The smallest number plotted is $5\frac{1}{2}$ and the largest number is $8\frac{1}{2}$. The range is 3.

18. $\frac{1}{2}, 1\frac{5}{8}$: $2\frac{1}{2} - \frac{3}{2}$ is already given as $1\frac{1}{8}$. Inside the parentheses convert the $\frac{2}{3}$ to $\frac{4}{6}$. Then you can do $\frac{4}{6} - \frac{1}{6} = \frac{3}{6} = \frac{1}{2}$. The first space is $\frac{1}{2}$. Then $1\frac{1}{8} + \frac{1}{2} = 1\frac{5}{8}$. The second space is $1\frac{5}{8}$.

19. B: Point T is equal to $2\frac{2}{3}$ and S is equal to 4. Perform all of the equations to figure out which one produces a number that is not on the number line. 2T-S= $2(2\frac{2}{3})$-4= $1\frac{1}{3}$ which is not on the number line.

20. Part A: C: There are a total of 8 spaces on the spinner all of equal size. There are 6 spaces that are 12 or greater. $\frac{6}{8} = \frac{3}{4}$.

Part B: $\frac{9}{16}$: The first time the probability was $\frac{3}{4}$ and the second time the probability is also $\frac{3}{4}$. The probability of it happening both times though is $\frac{3}{4} \times \frac{3}{4}$ which is $\frac{9}{16}$.

21. $7.13: If he buys each toy for $4.10 and then has another $1.30 in it, then he has a total of $5.40 in each toy. He marks it up 32% to sell it so his sales price is $5.40(1.32)=$7.128≈ $7.13.

22. A: Complementary angles sum to 90 degrees. Since Angle B measures 28°, Angle A measures 90° − 28°, or 62°.

23. A: Similar polygons must have congruent corresponding angles and proportional corresponding sides. Both requirements must be fulfilled in order to declare similarity in polygons.

24. D: One point is at (-3, 3) and the other is at (5, 3). So, they are at a distance of 8. Since each square is equal to 3 feet they are 24 feet apart.

25. A: If it takes him $\frac{2}{5}$ of a minute to dribble $\frac{2}{3}$ of the field then divide by 2 to get $\frac{1}{5}$ of a minute for $\frac{1}{3}$ of the field. Then you can multiply by 3 to get $\frac{3}{3}$ of the field in $\frac{3}{5}$ of a minute. $\frac{3}{5}$ of a minute equals 36 seconds.

26. C: If he puts a tire on that is 2 inches thick then that adds 4 inches to the overall diameter. Now the radius is 12 inches. The formula for circumference is $2\pi r$. 2 times 12π is 24π.

27. B: A reflection of a figure across the y-axis is achieved by finding the additive inverse of each x-value. The y-values will not change. Therefore, the vertices of the reflected figure are $(-4, 7)$, $(-9, 7)$, $(-2, 3)$, and $(-11, 3)$.

28. B: A regular heptagon has equal side lengths. Thus, an estimate for the perimeter can be computed by rounding the given side length and multiplying by 7 (the number of sides of a heptagon); 9.2 can be rounded to 9, and 9 × 7 =63. Thus, the best estimate for the perimeter of the heptagon is 63 cm.

29. C: The area of a parallelogram can be calculated using the formula $A = bh$. The length of the base of the parallelogram is 18 cm, and the height is 8 cm. Thus, the area is equal to 18 × 8 cm², or 144 cm².

30. D: The given triangle has a base equal to 4 units and a height equal to 6 units. Thus, the area of the triangle is equal to $\frac{1}{2}(4)(6)$ square units, or 12 square units.

31 The correct answer is **576**. The box is a rectangular prism, and the amount of available space inside the box is synonymous with the volume of the box. The volume of a rectangular prism is calculated by finding the product of the length, width, and height. Thus, the volume of the box is equal to 12 in × 8 in × 6 in, or 576 cubic inches.

32. D: The distance around the pothole indicates the circumference of the pothole. The circumference of a circle can be determined by using the formula $C = \pi d$, where C represents the circumference and d represents the diameter. The diameter of the pothole is 18 inches (9 × 2). Substituting a diameter of 18 inches and 3.14 for the value of pi gives the following: $C = 3.14(18)$, or 56.52. Thus, the distance around the pothole is equal to 56.52 inches.

33. B: The area of a trapezoid can be found by using the formula $A = \frac{1}{2}(b_1 + b_2)h$, where b_1 and b_2 represent the lengths of the bases and h represents the height of the trapezoid. Substituting the given base lengths and height reveals the following: $A = \frac{1}{2}(7 + 10)5$, which equals 42.5. Thus, the area of the trapezoid is 42.5 cm².

34. D: The sample space of rolling each die is 6. Thus, the sample space of rolling two dice is equal to the product of the sample spaces. 6 × 6 = 36; therefore, the sample space is equal to 36.

35. C: Flipping a coin one time has a sample space equal to 2, i.e., T or H. Flipping a coin 2 times has a sample space equal to 4, i.e., TT, HH, TH, HT. Flipping a coin 3 times has a sample space of 8, i.e., TTT, HHH, THT, HTH, TTH, HHT, THH, HTT. Notice that 2 is equal to 2^1, 4 is equal to 2^2, and 8 is equal to 2^3. The sample space of flipping a coin 9 times is equal to 2^9, or 512.

36. B: The events are independent since the spin of a spinner does not have an effect on the outcome of the flip of a coin. The probability of two independent events can be found using the formula $P(A \text{ and } B) = P(A) \cdot P(B)$. The probability of landing on a number less than 5 is $\frac{4}{8}$ since there are 4 possible numbers less than 5 (1, 2, 3, and 4). The probability of getting tails is $\frac{1}{2}$. The probability of landing on a number less than 5 and getting tails is $\frac{4}{8} \cdot \frac{1}{2}$, which equals $\frac{4}{16}$, or $\frac{1}{4}$.

37. C: Translation of the value of the nth term indicates the value will be 4 less than 6 times the position of the number, or n. The expression "6 times n" is written as 6n; subtraction of 4 from this expression gives $6n - 4$. Thus, the value of the nth term, or a_n, is written as $a_n = 6n - 4$.

38. C: A triangle with a base of 11 inches and a height of 9 inches has an area equal to $\frac{1}{2}(11)(9)$, or 49.5; an area of 49.5 square inches is greater than 49 square inches but less than 52 square inches. Therefore, she should use the dimensions of 11 inches and 9 inches.

39. D: The events are independent since Ann replaces the first marble drawn. The probability of two independent events can be found using the formula $P(A \text{ and } B) = P(A) \cdot P(B)$. The probability of pulling out a yellow marble is $\frac{8}{18}$. The probability of pulling out a green marble after the yellow marble has been replaced is $\frac{1}{18}$. The probability that Ann pulls out a yellow marble and then a green marble is $\frac{8}{18} \cdot \frac{1}{18}$, which equals $\frac{8}{324}$, which reduces to $\frac{2}{81}$.

40. B: The line graph shows the largest number of flights made during a month as 79 with the smallest number of flights made during a month as 54. The range is equal to the difference between the largest number of flights and smallest number of flights, i.e., 79 – 54 = 25. Therefore, the range is equal to 25.

41. D: A square pyramid has four triangular faces and a square base. Each side of the square has a triangle attached to it; since there are four sides on a square, there are four triangular faces on a square pyramid.

42. A: The percentages of each type of tree are as follows: Apple tree – 20%; Peach tree – 44%; Fig tree – 29%, and Pear tree – 7%. The circle graph for Choice A accurately represents these percentages.

43. A: The median can be determined using any of the given graphical representations. However, a box-and-whiskers plot actually includes a line drawn for the median, thus clearly indicating the value of the median.

44. The correct answer is 304. The median number of minutes can be determined by listing the number of minutes in order from least to greatest and calculating the average of the two middle values. The number of minutes can be written in ascending order as 255, 289, 291, 302, 306, 322,

411, and 418. The two middle values are 302 and 306. The average of these values can be determined by writing $\frac{302+306}{2}$, which equals 304. Thus, the median number of minutes is 304.

45. B: The average number (or mean) of incoming freshmen can be calculated by summing the numbers of incoming freshmen and dividing by the total number of years (or 10). Thus, the mean can be calculated by evaluating $\frac{76,146}{10}$, which equals 7,614.6. Since a fraction of a person cannot occur, the mean can be rounded to 7,615 freshmen.

46. B: First calculate Tina's pace. It takes her 36 minutes or .6 of an hour to walk 2.2 miles. So, divide her distance by .6 hours to get her miles per hour, which rounds to 3.67. Then repeat the process to find Josie's pace. Divide 1.9 by .5 to get 3.8 miles per hour.

Science

Scientific Method

The Steps of the Scientific Method

1. Find a topic to investigate. Usually this is in the form of a question. For example, what is the effect of the pH level of the soil on plants?
2. Gather information about the topic. Read books. Search for information on the Internet. Ask an expert. Narrow the broad topic into a specific topic. For example, what is the effect of the pH level of the soil on the growth of grass?
3. Form a hypothesis or an educated guess. Try to answer the question based on the information that was gathered during the research. For example, I think that grass will grow the tallest in a soil that is slightly basic.
4. Design and perform an experiment to test the hypothesis. Experiments have an independent variable, dependent variable, several constants and a control if possible. For example, the type of containers, soil, and grass plants as well as the amount of water and sunlight are the same for every trial of the experiment. Only the pH of the soil varies or changes.
5. Record the data during the experiment. Then study or analyze the data to determine the relationship between the independent variable and the dependent variable. This usually includes tables, charts, and graphs.
6. State the conclusion. Do the results support or contradict the original hypothesis?

Purpose and design of a good experiment

An experiment tests the hypothesis to discover if the hypothesis is true or false. An experiment includes an independent variable, a dependent variable, a control if possible, and several constants. The independent variable is the factor that is changed or varied during the experiment. The dependent variable is the factor that is measured during the experiment. The control is the group of the experiment that is not under the influence of the independent variable. The control is used for comparison. For example, for the hypothesis, "If grass is planted in soil with a slightly basic pH, then the grass will grow the tallest," the independent variable is the pH of the soil. The dependent variable is the height of the grass plant. The constants are factors that remain the same for all trials of the experiment including the control. A good experiment has numerous trials at each variation of the independent variable.

<u>Example</u>

Describe an experiment to test the hypothesis, "If grass is planted in soil with a slightly basic pH, then the grass will grow the tallest."

Hypothesis - If grass is planted in soil with a slightly basic pH, then the grass will grow the tallest.

The independent variable is the pH of the soil. The dependent variable is the height of the grass plants. The constants include the type of pot, type of soil, type of grass seed, temperature, humidity, and the amount of water and sunlight. Forty grass seeds are divided into four groups of ten. Group 1 (the control group) is planted in neutral soil. Group 2 is planted in slightly basic soil. Group 3 is planted in a more basic soil. Group 4 is planted in a slightly acidic soil. The heights of the plants are recorded in millimeters every three days for six weeks.

ACT Aspire Reasoning Test

1. ***Don't be scared by science terms or jargon.*** For many of the passages, you might not need to completely understand what is written in the paragraphs. Many of the questions are based only on your ability to read and take information from the graphs, charts, tables, figures, or illustrations.
2. ***The easiest questions usually come right after the passages.*** After quickly reading the passage and skimming the charts or illustrations, see if you can answer the first question from each passage.
3. ***Keep moving.*** Don't spend more than one minute on any question. Keep moving. The easy questions are worth as many points as the harder questions. By spending too much time on the harder questions, you will miss the chance to gain points by answering the easy questions associated with passages you will never even read before the time is up.
4. ***Work on the type of passages you think are the easiest first.*** Be prepared. Know the types of passages and questions covered on this test. Read the passages you feel the most comfortable with first.
5. ***Look for patterns or trends.*** When you read through the passage and glance over the charts and figures, look for patterns or trends. As one variable increases, does the other variable increase or decrease? How does changing one factor affect another factor?

Topics and types of passages covered on the ACT Aspire Science Reasoning Test

The ACT Aspire Science Reasoning Test covers a variety of science topics, including biology such as information about what affects the growth of plants, chemistry such as the pH scale, physics such as the effects of forces on motion, geology such as the different types of minerals, and astronomy such as information about the planets. Students are not expected to know specific or detailed knowledge of each topic. Instead, this test is designed to test your ability to read a scientific passage and find information from the charts, tables, graphs, and illustrations provided with the passage. Difficult terms are usually defined in the passage. Formulas are usually provided.

The ACT Aspire Science Reasoning Test includes three types of passages: data representation, research summaries, and conflicting viewpoints. In the data representation passages, a paragraph or paragraphs with charts, tables, figures, or illustrations are provided about a specific science topic. Students are expected to understand the passage and interpret the information in the chart, graphs, and other visual representations. In the research summary passages, details regarding an experiment and the data from that experiment are provided. Students need to understand, analyze, and interpret graphs and tables. Students need to understand the design of the experiment and interpret the results of the experiment. Students may be asked to make predictions or inferences. In the conflicting viewpoint passages, two or more opinions are presented about a scientific topic. Students need to recognize similarities and differences between the viewpoints.

ACT Aspire Science Reasoning Test

Types of questions on the ACT Aspire Science Reasoning Test

Each passage contains a paragraph and usually charts, tables, graphs, illustrations, or figures. This test is designed to test your ability to understand and use the information that is presented in the graphs and charts. To answer a question, you may simply need to read a term from a table or read data from a graph. The more difficult questions may ask for you to recognize patterns or trends. You may need to combine information from the graphs and charts in order to answer a question. Complex math calculations are not required. Usually you can use estimation to get a close answer and then select from the answers provided in the answer choices. You may have to draw inferences or make predictions from graphs and figures or interpret coordinating tables.

Strategies for approaching the data representation passages

Tips for the Data Representation Passages

1. ***Don't be afraid of science passages.*** You don't have to completely understand the passages to answer the questions. Even if the terms and concepts seem complex, the questions are usually pretty straightforward.
2. ***Usually the easiest questions are first.*** After quickly reading the passage and skimming the charts or illustrations, see if you can answer the first question associated with each passage. Usually the easiest questions are first.
3. ***Keep moving!*** Don't spend more than one minute on any particular question. If you don't know the answer, guess and move on. By spending too much time on the harder questions, you will miss the opportunity to gain points by answering the easy questions associated with passages you will never reach before the time is up.
4. ***Restate the problem in your own words.*** Ask yourself what information is needed. Find the information you need to answer the question.
5. ***Look for patterns.*** When you read through the passage and glance over the charts and figures, look for patterns or trends. Does one variable increase as another variable increases? Or does one variable decrease as another variable increases? Is there a direct or inverse relationship or variation? Is there a pattern? Are there any highs (maximums) or lows (minimums)?
6. ***Stick with the information in the passage.*** Don't use any outside science knowledge in answering the actual question. This science knowledge may help you understand the passage, but all the answers should be in the passage or inferred from the passage.

Example

Partial Passage and Information from Diagram of Human Skeleton: An adult skeleton has 206 bones. The skeleton has two major divisions: the axial skeleton and the appendicular skeleton. Bones in the leg and foot include the femur, patella, tibia, fibula, tarsals, metatarsals, and phalanges. Bones in the arms and hand include the humerus, radius, ulna, carpals, metacarpals, and phalanges.

Question: Which of the following bones is not associated with the leg?

a. Femur

b. Tibia

c. Patella

d. Radius

Suggested Approach: Study the diagram of the skeleton. The radius is a bone in the lower arm. The femur, tibia, and patella are located in the leg. Therefore, choice C is correct.

Example

Partial Passage: Calcium is needed for healthy bones and teeth. Calcium is stored in the bones. By the time a person is a young adult, his or her bone mass is the greatest it will ever be. This is called the peak bone mass. As a person becomes an older adult, his or her bone mass decreases

- 94 -

significantly. *Shown in the graph*: Bone mass versus age in years for males and females. Highest point on graph for males is near 30 years old and for females near 35 years old.

Question: At approximately what age do males reach their peak bone mass?

    a. 10

    b. 20

    c. 30

    d. 50

Suggested Approach: This question can be answered without even reading the passage. Often the first question following a passage is the simplest and can be answered from the accompanying graphs or charts. According to the figure, males reach their peak bone mass at approximately age 30. Females peak around age 35. Therefore, choice C is correct.

Research Summary Passages

What to expect in the research summary passages

In the research summary passages, details regarding an experiment and the data from that experiment are provided. Students need to understand, analyze, and interpret graphs and tables. Students need understand the design of the experiment and interpret the results of the experiment. Students may be asked to make predictions or inferences or to extrapolate. When reading about the experiment, ask these questions. What is being tested? Why is it being tested? What are the variables? What factors stay the same? Identify the independent variable and the dependent variable. Try to determine the relationship between these variables. Is there a direct relationship? Is there an inverse relationship? Be prepared to interpret data points and extrapolate data from tables and graphs. Remember, many of the questions can be answered by interpreting the charts and graphs without even reading the passage. When studying the graphs and charts, be sure to read all captions, keys, and labels. Identify axes and units.

Example

Partial Experiment Passage: Students studied the effect of the pH level of the soil on the growth of grass. The pH of the soil was varied between a pH of 6.0 and 8.0.Ten identical grass seeds were planted in each pot. The seeds were watered with equal amounts for a total of 14 days. The height of each grass plant was measured after 14 days and recorded in millimeters.

Question: Which of the following is the independent variable for this experiment?

    a. The type of grass seed

    b. The amount of water

    c. The pH of the soil

    d. The height of the grass

Suggested Approach: The independent variable is the variable that is changed or varied by the students performing the experiment. The dependent variable is the variable that is measured. In this experiment, the students varied the pH of the soil. The height of the grass plants was measured. Therefore, choice C is correct.

- 95 -

Conflicting Viewpoint Passage

What to expect in the conflicting viewpoint passage

In the conflicting viewpoint passages, two or more opinions are presented about a scientific topic. Usually the opinions have very specific differences. The opinions or viewpoints also share a few common ideas. Students need to recognize similarities and differences between the viewpoints. Some questions will cover specific details about the viewpoints. Students might be asked to make inferences or draw reasonable conclusions from the information that is provided. Some questions may ask which statements both or all of the viewpoints agree with or who might agree or disagree with a particular statement. Only one of these types of passages is on this test.

Tips for Approaching the Conflicting Viewpoint Passage
1. ***It doesn't matter who's right!*** When reading the opposing or conflicting viewpoints, stick to the facts in the passage. Don't worry about who you think is right or wrong.
2. ***Ignore your own opinion!*** Your viewpoint doesn't matter. Just read the passage and get the needed information to answer the questions.
3. ***Take shorthand notes.*** Jot down or underline the information that supports each viewpoint. Jot down or circle key points of each viewpoint. Only use information that is stated in the viewpoints.
4. ***Look for similarities and differences.*** Ask yourself how the conflicting viewpoints disagree about the same concept or explain the same concept.

Example

Partial Passage: The Endangered Species Act provides for the conservation of ecosystems that contain the habitats of endangered species. *Scientist A:* The Endangered Species Act is effective is restoring species that were previously endangered. The act makes the public aware and concerned about endangered species. *Scientist B:* While the Endangered Species Act is effective in restoring species that were previously endangered, the act is too expensive to implement and too extreme.

Question: Which of the following statements would both of the scientists agree with?

   a. The Endangered Species Act is too expensive to implement.

   b. The Endangered Species Act is effective in restoring species.

   c. The Endangered Species Act is too extreme as it is currently written.

   d. Man has a responsibility to preserve rare species at all costs.

Suggested Approach: Since the scientists have extremely different viewpoints, the statement they might both agree with will be a general statement about the topic. These statements are often located in the beginning of the passages. In the opening sentences, both scientists state that the Endangered Species Acts has been effective in restoring species. Therefore, choice B is correct.

Example

Partial Passage: The Endangered Species Act provides for the conservation of ecosystems that contain the habitats of endangered species. *Scientist A:* This act is responsible for maintaining the natural habitat of many species. It is man's responsibility to preserve rare species at all costs. The Endangered Species Act has saved many animals, including alligators, whooping cranes, and bald eagles.

Question: Which of the following statements would Scientist A be most likely to disagree with?

    a. The Endangered Species Act helped save the bald eagle.

    b. The Endangered Species Act preserves habitats of numerous species.

    c. The Endangered Species Act should be enforced at all costs.

    d. The Endangered Species Act is too expensive and too extreme.

Suggested Approach: Before reading any of the questions, read through all the passages. Underline key points and jot down notes in the margins. When you see the question is specifically about Scientist A, glance over the underlined parts and notes from that passage. Scientist A stresses the importance of preserving species regardless of the costs. Therefore, choice D is correct.

Practice Test

Practice Questions

Use the following information for Questions 1-6.

Reading Weather Maps

A weather map shows the weather conditions over a large area for a particular period of time. Weather maps typically show high and low pressure regions, precipitation, and temperature. High pressure regions are associated with fair weather. Low pressure regions are associated with rain and storms. Warm and cold fronts are also shown on weather maps. Cold fronts often precede heavy rain. Cold fronts may bring cumulonimbus clouds and heavy precipitation. Thunderstorms may occur along the leading edge of a cold front. When looking at a weather map, cities behind a cold front may experience rain as shown by a shaded region. Cold fronts usually move from west to east across the United States. Warm fronts often precede moderate rain. When a warm front moves into a region, the warm air rises up over cooler stationary air forming nimbostratus clouds and bringing moderate precipitation.

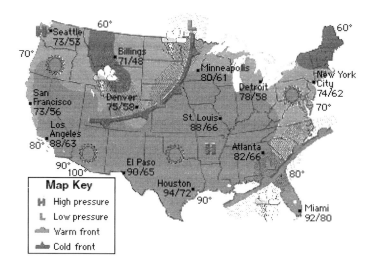

Figure 1

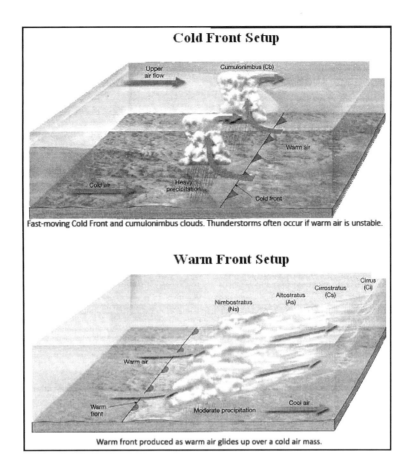

Cold Front Setup

Upper air flow

Cumulonimbus (Cb)

Warm air

Cold air

Heavy precipitation

Cold front

Fast-moving Cold Front and cumulonimbus clouds. Thunderstorms often occur if warm air is unstable.

Warm Front Setup

Cirrus (Ci)

Cirrostratus (Cs)

Altostratus (As)

Nimbostratus (Ns)

Warm air

Warm front

Moderate precipitation

Cool air

Warm front produced as warm air glides up over a cold air mass.

Figure 2

1. According to this weather map, which city is currently experiencing rain?

   a. Houston
   b. Denver
   c. Miami
   d. Detroit

2. According to this map, which city will most likely experience rain in the next few days?

   a. El Paso
   b. Los Angeles
   c. Minneapolis
   d. New York City

3. According to this map, which city is near a high pressure region?

   a. Seattle
   b. Atlanta
   c. Billings
   d. Denver

4. According to Figure 1, which type of cloud is not associated with a warm front?

    a. Cirrostratus
    b. Altostratus
    c. Nimbostratus
    d. Cumulonimbus

5. According to the information from the passage, which type of cloud is associated with heavy precipitation?

    a. Cirrostratus
    b. Altostratus
    c. Cirrus
    d. Cumulonimbus

6. Which of the following best describes the weather near Seattle?

    a. Fair and sunny
    b. Overcast and cloudy
    c. Light rains
    d. Heavy thunderstorms

Use the following information for Questions 7-12.

Kinetic energy and potential energy

Matter possesses both kinetic and potential energy. Kinetic energy is energy of motion. Kinetic energy may appear in many forms, such as light, sound, and heat or thermal energy. Potential energy is energy of position or configuration. The means potential energy is stored energy. Potential energy includes gravitational, chemical, and elastic potential energy. See Figure 1. The kinetic energy of an object is related to the velocity of the particles of the object. If the particles move or vibrate fast, the kinetic energy increases. Kinetic energy is indicated by the temperature of an object. The higher an object's temperature, the more kinetic energy it possesses. Energy can be transferred from one object to another object. This potential energy indicates that the matter may move. If the potential energy is converted to kinetic energy, the object may move. For example, a stretched rubber band possesses elastic potential energy. The potential energy is due to the force that is applied to the rubber band. When the rubber band is released, this potential energy is changed into kinetic energy. The gravitational potential energy of an object is related to its height above the ground. The higher an object is above ground level, the higher the object's gravitational potential energy. When an object moves to a lower height, its gravitational potential energy is converted to kinetic energy.

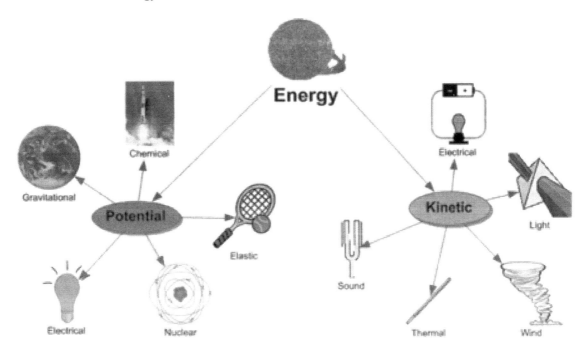

Figure 1

7. Which of the following is an example of elastic potential energy?

    a. Gasoline in a lawnmower
    b. A bowstring pulled back
    c. A rolling bowling ball
    d. Light from the sun

8. Which of the following has the greatest gravitational potential energy?

    a. A baseball lying on the ground
    b. A TV remote on a low coffee table
    c. A book on a high shelf
    d. A kitten running across the yard

9. Which of the following objects possesses the least amount of kinetic energy?

    a. A baseball travelling at 90 mph.
    b. A baseball rolling slowly across the ground.
    c. A baseball falling from the top of a building.
    d. A baseball lying on the pitcher's mound.

10. A rollercoaster at the top of the tallest hill starts to move down the hill. Which of the following correctly describes this situation in terms of kinetic and potential energy?

    a. Gravitational potential energy is being converted to chemical potential energy.
    b. Kinetic energy is being converted to gravitational potential energy.
    c. Gravitational potential energy is being converted to kinetic energy.
    d. Chemical potential energy is being converted to kinetic energy.

11. At which of the following temperatures would 100 ml of water have the greatest amount of kinetic energy?

    a. -2°C
    b. 62°C
    c. 0°C
    d. 25°C

12. According to the Figure 1, which of the following is most likely true concerning sound?

    a. Sound is an example of kinetic energy.
    b. Sound is an example of potential energy.
    c. Sound is an example of both kinetic energy and potential energy.
    d. Sound is an example of neither kinetic energy nor potential energy.

Use the following information for Questions 13-18.

The Protist Kingdom includes many living organisms that consist of single cells. The Protist Kingdom is divided into several phyla, including the phyla listed in Figure 1. Protists are more complex than bacteria and are found in many different types of environments. While protists are great in variety, they do share many similar characteristics. Although most protists consist of only one cell, each of the organisms much carry out the functions necessary to maintain life, such as movement, processing food, secreting wastes, and reproduction. Protists include euglenas, amoebas, and paramecia. Euglenas are flagellates that move by means of flagella or whip-like structures that are attached near their front end. Euglenas can be found in puddles and ponds. Euglenas contain chlorophyll and are capable of both consuming food and producing food by photosynthesis. Amoebas are pseudopods that move by means of "false feet" or extensions from the body that continually change its body outline. Amoebas can be found in wet soil or mud near decaying plants. Some amoebas can cause an illness in humans known as dysentery, which causes severe diarrhea. Paramecia are ciliates that move by means of cilia or tiny hair-like structures that surround the entire outer body. Paramecia can be found in ponds, rivers, and lakes. Some types of paramecia form a symbiotic relationship with green algae in which both organisms benefit each other.

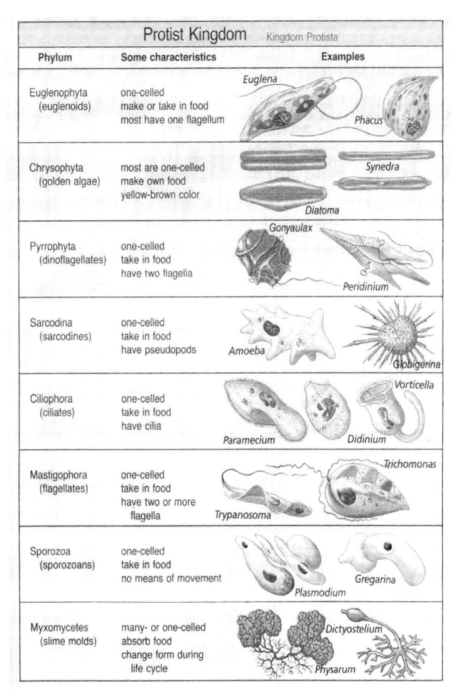

Figure 1

13. According to Figure 1, to which of the following phyla would a protist that moves by means of "false feet" belong?

   a. *Euglenophyta*
   b. *Ciliophora*
   c. *Mastigophora*
   d. *Sarcodina*

14. Which of the following protists would most likely be yellow-brown in color?

   a. Euglena
   b. Amoeba
   c. Diatoma
   d. Plasmodium

15. Which of the following protists does not move by means of a flagellum?

   a. Vorticella
   b. Phacus
   c. Trypanosoma
   d. Euglena

16. Which of the following protists contains chlorophyll?

   a. Peridinium
   b. Euglena
   c. Gregarina
   d. Amoeba

17. Which of the following single-celled organisms has no means of movement?

   a. Amoeba
   b. Plasmodium
   c. Paramecium
   d. Euglena

18. Which of the following characteristics do the euglenas, amoebas, and paramecium not have in common?

   a. All of these organisms can make their own food.
   b. All of these organisms have a means of reproduction.
   c. All of these organisms can be found in moist habitats.
   d. All of these organisms are single-celled organisms.

Use the following information for Questions 19-24.

Plant growth is affected by the pH of the soil. Soil may be acidic, neutral, or basic (alkaline). The pH scale ranges from 0 to 14, with 0 indicating a strong acid and 14 indicating a strong base. If a soil sample is neutral, the pH level is 7. If a soil sample is acidic, the pH level is less than 7. If a soil sample is basic, the pH level is greater than 7. Soil pH is compared to the known pH levels of several common substances in Figure 1. Some plants such as grass thrive in soil with a pH level slightly less than 7. A pH of 6.5 is considered too low for grass to grow well. A pH greater than 7.5 is considered too high for grass to grow well. The pH level of soil can be raised if necessary by adding lime. If the pH level of soil is too high, sulfur can be added to lower the pH. Landscapers use test kits to sample

- 104 -

soil to determine which treatment is necessary. The use of a soil chart determines the amount of lime or sulfur to add to reach the ideal pH for a particular grass.

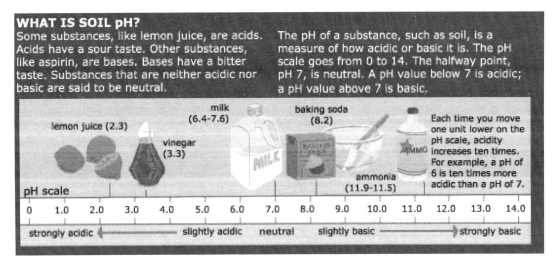

Figure 1

19. Which of the following common substances most closely matches the pH level needed for grass to grow well?

    a. Vinegar
    b. Milk
    c. Baking soda
    d. Ammonia

20. Which of the following pH values indicated that a soil is slightly basic?

    a. 7.0
    b. 6.5
    c. 14.0
    d. 7.2

21. A landscaper determines that the soil in the area where grass is to be planted is too acidic. Which of the following is the landscaper's best option to raise the pH of the soil?

    a. Add lime to the soil
    b. Add vinegar to the soil
    c. Add sulfur to the soil
    d. Add milk to the soil

Experiment 1

Students studied the effect of the pH level of the soil on the growth of grass. The pH of the soil was varied between a pH of 6.0 and 8.0. The proper pH of each soil sample was obtained by using a pH test kit to test the soil and then adding the appropriate amounts of lime or sulfur to reach the needed pH for each trial.

An equal amount of soil was placed in five separate flower pots. The soil in the pots varied in pH from 6.0 to 8.0.Ten identical grass seeds were planted in each pot according to the package directions. The seeds were watered with equal amounts every day for a total of 14 consecutive days. The height of each grass plant was measured after 14 days and recorded in millimeters. The average heights for the plants in each soil pH are shown in Table 1.

Table 1	
pH	Average Grass Height in Millimeters
6.0	85
6.5	365
7.0	375
7.5	104
8.0	85

22. Which of the following is the independent variable for this experiment?
    a. The type of grass seed
    b. The amount of water
    c. The pH of the soil
    d. The height of the grass

23. Which of the following is a list containing only constants of the experiment?
    a. Type of seed, amount of water, amount of soil
    b. Type of seed, height of grass, pH of soil
    c. Amount of water, amount of soil, pH of soil
    d. Amount of water, amount of soil, height of grass

24. During this experiment, which pH level of soil produced grass with the greatest average height?
    a. 6.5
    b. 7.0
    c. 7.5
    d. 6.0

Use the following information for Questions 25-29.

Endangered species refers to a group of animals or plants that are at risk of becoming extinct. The Endangered Species Act of 1973 is an environmental law that provides for the conservation of ecosystems that contain the habitats of endangered of threatened species.

Scientist A

Scientist A states that the Endangered Species Act is effective in restoring species that were previously endangered. Simply having the act makes the public aware and therefore concerned about threatened and endangered species. This act is responsible for significant ecosystem preservation in the United States by maintaining the natural habitat of many species. This act has aided in the establishment of laws and regulations concerning the hunting and capture of many species. It is man's responsibility to preserve rare species at all costs. Without the Endangered Species Act, numerous species will become extinct due to habitat destruction and hunting. For example, the passenger pigeon was once known across North America for vast flocks of thousands or hundreds of thousands and sometimes millions. The passenger pigeon became extinct when forests were cut down and thousands were shot for sport. The Endangered Species Act has saved many animals, including alligators, whooping cranes, bald eagles, grizzly bears, and wolves, from becoming extinct.

Scientist B

Scientist B states that while the Endangered Species Act is effective in restoring species that were previously endangered, the act is too expensive to implement and too extreme. Restricting the use of land to preserve natural habitats for rare species can have a negative effect on the community, tourism, and job opportunities. Society must weigh the need to preserve rare species with the costs and lost job opportunities. For example, when a spotted owl was listed as threatened in 1990, the surrounding timber industry was seriously affected. Many acres of forest were declared off limits to preserve the owl's natural habitat. This caused thousands of loggers and mill workers to lose their jobs. Similar issues have arisen with preserving the habitats of dolphins, whales, tortoises, elk, flying squirrels, and many other animals, affecting various industries, including mining, drilling for oil and natural gas, and the construction of hydroelectric dams.

25. Which of the following statements would both of the scientists agree with?

    a. The Endangered Species Act is too expensive to implement.
    b. The Endangered Species Act is effective in restoring species.
    c. The Endangered Species Act is too extreme as it is currently written.
    d. Man has a responsibility to preserve rare species at all costs.

26. Which of the following birds is extinct?

    a. Passenger pigeon
    b. Bald eagle
    c. Peregrine falcon
    d. Whooping crane

27. Which of the following statements would Scientist A be most likely to disagree with?

    a. The Endangered Species Act helped save the bald eagle.
    b. The Endangered Species Act preserves habitats of numerous species.
    c. The Endangered Species Act should be enforced at all costs.
    d. The Endangered Species Act is too expensive and too extreme.

28. Which of the following statements would Scientist B be most likely to disagree with?

    a. The Endangered Species Act has helped save endangered species.
    b. Man must weigh the cost when deciding which species to preserve.
    c. Man has a responsibility to preserve species no matter the effect on job opportunities.
    d. Industries such coal mining and gold mining provide numerous job opportunities.

29. Which of the following statements concerning the Endangered Species Act is not true?

    a. The Endangered Species Act helps preserve habitats.
    b. The Endangered Species Act helps to maintain mining and logging jobs.
    c. The Endangered Species Act helps establish hunting regulations.
    d. The Endangered Species Act helps to preserve endangered and threatened species.

Use the following information for Questions 30-35.

Passage

Solar cells, or photovoltaic cells, convert the sun's energy that reaches the Earth in the form of light into usable electrical energy. This electrical energy can be utilized immediately or stored in batteries to use later. Solar cells can be linked together to form larger solar panels. Solar cells are made of silicon, which is the second most abundant element in the Earth's crust. While silicon is abundantly found in the Earth, it is expensive to convert into the form needed for the production of solar cells. This makes the use of solar energy expensive. Many types of solar cells are being produced. Three types of common solar cells include monocrystalline solar cells, polycrystalline solar cells, and amorphous solar cells. Monocrystalline solar cells are the most efficient, with an energy conversion rate of approximately 18 percent. However, these are also the most expensive. Polycrystalline solar cells have an energy conversion rate of approximately 13 percent and are cheaper than monocrystalline solar cells. Amorphous solar cells are the least efficient, with an energy conversion rate of approximately 10 percent. These are the cheapest of the common types of solar cells. Even the rarest, most expensive solar cells, such as the gallium arsenide solar cell, only have an energy conversion rate of approximately 45 percent. In order to maximize solar cell efficiency, the solar cells need to be oriented perpendicularly to the sun's incoming rays. The angle that the solar cell makes with the sun's incoming rays is called the angle of incidence. Solar trackers follow the course of the sun throughout the day and adjust the angle of the solar panels. This optimizes solar cell performance, allowing them to produce as much electricity as possible at any given point of the day.

Experiment

Students performed an experiment to determine the effect of the incidence of solar rays on the performance of a solar cell. The angle of incidence of the solar rays and the solar cells was varied in 15° increments from 0° to 90°. The voltage and amperage, or amount of current, were measured at each angle and recorded in Table 1. The output power of the solar cells was calculated at each angle using the formula:

$$Power = Voltage \times Current$$

in which the units for power, voltage, and current were watts, volts, and amperes, respectively. The output power for each angle was also recorded in Table 1.

Table 1			
Angle of Incidence	Voltage (V)	Current (Amps)	Power (Watts)
0°	0.337	1.20	0.404
15°	0.375	1.25	0.469
30°	0.415	1.30	0.540
45°	0.450	1.45	0.653
60°	0.475	1.55	0.736
75°	0.487	1.70	0.828
90°	0.500	1.85	0.925

30. What is the approximate highest energy conversion rate available in solar cells?

    a. 13 percent
    b. 45 percent
    c. 18 percent
    d. 10 percent

31. Which of the following types of solar cells is the cheapest?

    a. Amorphous solar cells
    b. Monocrystalline solar cells
    c. Polycrystalline solar cells
    d. Gallium arsenide solar cells

32. Students repeated the experiment with a different solar cell. At a 90° angle of incidence, the voltage was measured at 0.400 volts, and the current was measured at 1.80 amperes. What is the power output?

    a. 4.500 watts
    b. 1.400 watts
    c. 2.200 watts
    d. 0.720 watts

33. What was the amount of current output by the solar cell at an angle of incidence of 30°?

    a. 0.415 volts
    b. 0.540 watts
    c. 1.30 amperes
    d. 1.45 amperes

34. What is the relationship between angle of incidence and output power?

    a. As the angle of incidence increases, the output power decreases.
    b. As the angle of incidence increases, the output power increases.
    c. As the angle of incidence increases, the output power remains constant.
    d. As the angle of incidence increases, the output power fluctuates.

Use the following information for Questions 35-40.

Surface tension is a phenomenon of a liquid such as water, in which the attraction between the molecules at the surface causes the surface to act like a thin film or elastic sheet. Objects such as pins or needles often appear to float when laid gently on the surface of water, even though these objects have a greater density than water. Insects such as water striders appear to walk on water by the use of surface tension. Surface tension is due to the way the water molecules at the surface of a liquid are attracted to the neighboring water molecules located at the sides and underneath them. Since there is only air above these molecules, the individual water molecules at the surface of the water cohere or are attracted much more strongly to the nearby water molecules than to the gaseous molecules above the surface. Surface tension explains why water droplets are round. A sphere has the smallest surface area for a given volume. Due to the attraction of the water molecules with each other, the molecules are pulled into the smallest surface area possible, which is the spherical shape. The addition of a substance such as salt can affect the surface tension of water. The amount of salt that is added to the water is called salinity. As salt is added to the water, the water molecules are pushed apart and cohere to each other less.

Experiment 1

Students designed an experiment to determine the effect of temperature on the surface tension of distilled water. Temperatures were varied in 10° increments from 20°C to 60°C. To measure the surface tension, students used a 1 cm by 1 cm piece of aluminum foil placed gently on the surface of water. Individual rice grains were added one at a time until the foil sank. The results were recorded in Table 1.

Table 1	
The Effect of Temperature on the Surface Tension of Distilled Water	
Temperature °C	**Number of grains of rice**
20	17
30	15
40	12
50	10
60	8

Experiment 2

Students extended their experiment to test the effect of salinity on the surface tension of water. Students repeated the previous experiment using a solution of salt water in place of the distilled water. Students then plotted their data from both experiments in Figure 1.

Table 2	
The Effect of Temperature on the Surface Tension of Salt Water	
Temperature °C	**Number of grains of rice**
20	7
30	6
40	5
50	4
60	3

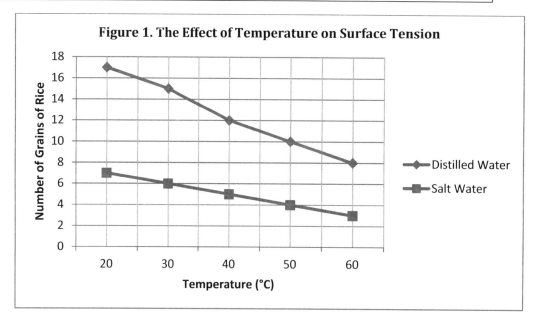

- 110 -

35. What is the relationship between the temperature and the surface tension of the distilled water?

    a. As temperature increases, surface tension increases and then decreases.
    b. As temperature increases, surface tension remains the same.
    c. As temperature increases, surface tension increases.
    d. As temperature increases, surface tension decreases.

36. Which of the following best describes the effect of salinity on surface tension?

    a. As salinity increases, surface tension remains the same.
    b. As salinity increases, surface tension decreases.
    c. As salinity increases, surface tension increases and then decreases.
    d. As salinity increase, surface tension increases.

37. Which of the following best describes why water droplets are spherical?

    a. Because they form the largest mass possible for a given volume
    b. Because they form the smallest mass possible for a given volume
    c. Because they form the largest surface area possible for a given volume
    d. Because they form the smallest surface area possible for a given volume

38. How many grains of rice would it most likely take to sink a 1 cm by 1cm piece of foil that is resting of the surface of distilled water at 45° C?

    a. 9
    b. 10
    c. 11
    d. 12

39. How many more grains did the foil hold on distilled water than on salt water at 50°C?

    a. 6
    b. 5
    c. 4
    d. 10

40. What is the dependent variable in *Experiment 2*?

    a. The type of rice used to sink the foil square
    b. The amount of water in the container
    c. The number of grains required to sink the foil square
    d. The temperature of the water in the container

Answers and Explanations

1. B: According to the map, Denver is located behind a cold front and is experiencing rain as indicated by the shading. Therefore, choice B is correct.

2. C: According to the passage, cold fronts bring rain. According to the weather map, Minneapolis will soon experience a cold front. Therefore, choice C is correct.

3. A: According to the map, regions of high pressure are indicated by a capital *H*. Seattle is near a region marked with a capital *H*. Therefore, choice A is correct.

4. D: According to Figure 1, nimbostratus, altostratus, cirrostratus, and cirrus clouds are associated with a warm front. Cumulonimbus clouds are associated with a cold front. Therefore, choice D is correct.

5. D: According to Figure 1, cold fronts bring heavy precipitation from cumulonimbus clouds. Therefore, choice D is correct.

6. A: From the map, Seattle is near a high pressure region. From the passage, areas near high pressure regions experience fair weather. Therefore, choice A is correct.

7. B: Elastic potential energy is due to an object's position relative to a force applied to the object. The gasoline lawnmower is an example of chemical potential energy. Both sunlight and a rolling bowling ball are examples of kinetic energy. A bowstring that is pulled back has elastic potential energy due to the force applied to the bowstring. Therefore, choice B is correct.

8. C: According to the passage, gravitational potential energy increases with an object's distance from the ground. Since the book is the highest from the ground level, the book has the greatest gravitational potential energy. Therefore, choice C is correct.

9. D: According to the passage, kinetic energy increases with velocity. It follows that kinetic energy decreases with a decrease in velocity. The baseball that is not moving has a velocity of zero, and should have the least amount of kinetic energy. Therefore, choice D is correct.

10. C: At the top of the tallest hill, the roller coaster has the most gravitational potential energy it can have on this track, since it is at the highest point it can possibly reach. As the roller coaster moves down the hill, this gravitational potential energy is converted to energy of motion or kinetic energy. Therefore, choice C is correct.

11. B: According to the passage, kinetic energy increases with temperature. The highest temperature should be associated with the highest kinetic energy. Therefore, choice B is correct.

12. A: According to Figure 1, sound is diagramed as a type of kinetic energy. Sound is not diagramed as a type of potential energy. Therefore, choice A is correct.

13. D: From the passage, pseudopods are described as "false feet." From Figure 1, protists with pseudopods are in the Phylum Sarcodina. Therefore, choice D is correct.

14. C: From Figure 1, protists in the Phylum Chrysophyta are yellow-brown in color. Diatoma are listed in Phylum Chrysophyta. Therefore, choice C is correct.

- 112 -

15. A: From the passage, euglenas move by means of flagella. From Figure 1, phacus, trypanosoma, and trichomonas also move by means of flagella. Vorticella is listed as a ciliophora, which is stated to move by means of cilia. Therefore, choice A is correct.

16. B: The passage states that the euglena contains chlorophyll. This is verified by Figure 1, which states the euglena can make its own food. Therefore, choice B is correct.

17. B: The passage states that the amoeba moves by pseudopods. The paramecium moves by means of cilia, and the euglena moves by means of a flagellum. In Figure 1, the plasmodium is listed in the phylum that has no form of movement. Therefore, choice B is correct.

18. A: According to the passage and Figure 1, of the protists listed only the euglena can make its own food. The euglena contains chlorophyll and can make its own food by photosynthesis. Therefore, choice A is correct.

19. B: According to the passage, grass grows well in soil that is slightly acidic. According to Figure 1, milk has a pH value of 6.4-7.6. Therefore, choice B is correct.

20. D: According to the passage and Figure 1, a pH value greater than 7 indicates that a soil is basic. A pH value of 14.0 would indicate the strongest base possible. A pH value of 7.2 is slightly above a pH value of neutral or 7.0. Therefore, choice D is correct.

21. A: According to the passage, the pH of the soil can be raised by adding lime. Therefore, choice A is correct.

22. C: The independent variable is the variable that is changed or varied by the students performing the experiment. In this experiment, the students varied the pH of the soil. Therefore, choice C is correct.

23. A: Controls are the constants of the experiment. Controls are the same for every trial. In this experiment, the type of seed, amount of water, and amount of soil were the same for all trials. Therefore, choice A is correct.

24. C: According to Table 1, the average height of the grass in the soil of pH 7.0 was 375 mm. This is the greatest height recorded in the table. Therefore, choice C is correct.

25. B: Both scientists state that the Endangered Species Acts has been effective in restoring species. Therefore, choice B is correct.

26. A: The bald eagle, peregrine falcon, and whooping crane are listed as being saved by the Endangered Species Act. The passenger pigeon is stated to be extinct. Therefore, choice A is correct.

27. D: Scientist A stresses the importance of preserving species regardless of the costs. Therefore, choice D is correct.

28. C: Scientist B speaks about the economic impact of the Endangered Species Act. Scientist B states that society must weigh the need to preserve rare species with the costs and lost job opportunities. Scientist B would not agree that man must preserve species no matter the effect on job opportunities. Therefore, choice C is correct.

29. B: The Endangered Species Act helps to preserve habitats of endangered and threatened species. As a result, land areas must be preserved from mining and logging, which threatens jobs instead of maintaining jobs. Therefore, choice B is correct.

30. B: According to the passage, even the rarest, most expensive solar cells only have an energy conversion rate of approximately 45%. Therefore, choice B is correct.

31. A: According to the passage, the amorphous solar cells are the least efficient and the cheapest of the common types of solar cells. Therefore, choice A is correct.

32. D: According to the passage, output power is calculated using the formula Power = Voltage X Current. Multiplying 0.400 volts by 1.80 amperes yields 0.720 watts. Therefore, choice D is correct.

33. C: According to Table 1, the current output at 30° is 1.30 amperes. Therefore, choice C is correct.

34. B: According to Table 1, as the angle of incidence increases, the output power increases. This can be seen by comparing the output power column to the angle of incidence column. Therefore, choice B is correct.

35. D: According to Figure 1, as temperature increases, the number of grains of rice held on the foil decreases. Since the number of grains of rice decreases, the surface tension decreases. Therefore, choice D is correct.

36. B: From Figure 1, the line representing the salt water lies below the line representing the distilled water. This means that at every temperature, the surface tension of the salt water was less than the surface tension of the distilled water. As salinity increases, surface tension decreases. Therefore, choice B is correct.

37. D: Water molecules are greatly attracted to each other and form the smallest surface area possible for each particular volume. A spherical shape has the smallest surface area for a given volume. Therefore, choice D is correct.

38. C: From Figure 1, at 45°C the line for the distilled water (top line) crosses midway between 10 grains and 12 grains. This means that at 45°C, it should take 11 grains of rice to sink the foil in distilled water. Therefore, choice C is correct.

39. A: The number of grains of rice required to sink the foil in the distilled water at 50°C was 10 grains. The number of grains of rice required to sink the foil in the salt water at 50°C was 4 grains. The foil square in the distilled water held 4 more grains of rice than the foil in the salt water. Therefore, choice A is correct.

40. C: The dependent variable is the variable that changes as the independent variable is changes. In *Experiment 2*, the independent variable was the temperature of the water. As the temperature of the water increased, the number of grains required to sink the foil decreased. This means the dependent variable is the number of grins required to sink the foil. Therefore, choice C is correct.

Reading

Literature

Explicit information

Explicit information includes facts and statements that are found directly in a passage or a story. It is not information that is hinted at or information you need to make a conclusion about. Explicit information may be found in many forms; it can be contained in a quote as well as in a description. It can be found in dialogue and in actions. This information can sometimes be used to support an inference. The answers to questions about explicit information are found through careful reading of the text. Attention is given to pertinent facts or other information. In fiction, details about characters, events, and setting can be both explicit and implicit.

Read the following excerpt and tell what information is explicit:

> Carlos didn't really speak Spanish. His parents often spoke to him in that language, which he understood, but he always replied in English. As a result, his Spanish pronunciation was very bad, and he had trouble picking the right word. But then he fell in love with Alicia, who didn't understand English. Carlos changed very quickly.

The explicit information in the excerpt is all about Carlos. The passage says that he didn't really speak Spanish. It says that while his parents spoke to him in Spanish and that he understood it, he always responded in English. It also says his Spanish pronunciation was bad and he didn't pick the right words. This is explicit information. So is the fact that Carlos fell in love with Alicia and that Carlos changed quickly.

Inference

An inference is the best guess a reader can make based on the information in a passage. An inference has to be based on what a reader knows from personal knowledge and what is stated in a passage or story. Inferences can be about people, things, or ideas. A good inference is supported by information and is the most likely conclusion that can be made based on the evidence in a story or text. Inferences are not like explicit information, which is clearly stated in a passage. A reader must put the hints together to come up with the best conclusion to make a successful inference.

Read the excerpt and the question that follows it. Answer the question and explain why it is correct.

> The great day had arrived and Jesse could hardly believe it. For a whole year he had saved. All through the winter and spring he had worked overtime. Now it was June 25 and he was on his way. He would have two full weeks in Paris.

Tell why you can conclude that Jesse is going on vacation.

You can draw the conclusion that Jesse is going on a summer vacation because the information in the passage says that the great day had arrived and that Jesse had saved for this a whole year. It also says he would have two full weeks in Paris. This is a logical conclusion based on the information in the passage. It is the best guess a reader can make from the information that he or she has read. Inferences are based on the information in a passage and they are the best guess that a reader can make based on that information

- 115 -

Determining the purpose of a text

It should be, for the most part, fairly easy to determine the purpose of a text. When reading, ask yourself whether the passage is teaching or instructing you about something, trying to appeal to your emotions, trying to convince you of something, or simply trying to entertain you. There are certain signs that a text is attempting to persuade the reader. The author will offer up an opinion and tell why she thinks this way. If a text is simply informative, it will have many facts that will give details about an event or person, but will not offer an opinion. Examples of texts that entertain are novels, short stories, and science fiction. Instructional manuals that come with equipment are clearly not persuasive.

Determining the theme of a passage

The theme of a passage is the message or broad idea of the passage. It is what the passage teaches the reader. It is the lesson or moral that the passage carries with it. The theme of a passage is often based on one of life's universal themes. Most themes are about life, society, or human nature. A theme is not usually stated explicitly. The reader must figure it out from the topic, information, or plot of a passage. The theme is often why a passage is written. It helps give a passage unity. The theme is created through the development of the story. The events of a story help shape the kind of theme the passage teaches. Oftentimes, the author does not tell you what the theme is. You have to figure it out.

Read the following and decide which represents the best theme of the excerpt.

> Jeanie arrived at the bake sale early. She bought the biggest cake at the sale. Sally had to work late. When she finally got to the sale, no cakes were left. She got only two cookies. She was lucky to get anything.

Tell why "The early bird gets the worm" describes the story's theme best.

This saying is the closest to the theme of the story. In the story we read that Jeanie arrived early at the bake sale and got the biggest cake. But when Sally arrived, all that was left were two cookies. The point of the story is that the early bird gets the worm—the worm in this case is a large cake. The theme is what the story is teaching the reader. It is the message the author wants to get across. This is the message of this passage. The reader needs to figure out the theme from what happens in a story.

Creating an objective summary of a passage

A summary must include the main ideas of a passage as well as the important details that support the main idea. It should be more than a general statement about what a passage is about. It should include vital events and other details that make the story unique and memorable. In order to make the summary objective, you must make sure to reflect what the passage is about. A summary puts the information in a short form. That is how summarizing is different from paraphrasing. Paraphrasing rewords the main idea and supporting ideas in greater detail; summaries do not. Summaries allow the reader to remember the main points of a passage and the important details.

Shaping a character with setting or plot

Setting or plot shapes character because each helps to define the situation that a character finds herself in. A character is limited to the setting of a story. For example, if a story takes place in a cold environment filled with snow and ice, this is certain to impact what actions a character can and will undertake. Similarly, the plot influences a character. What happens in the story directly affects what a character will do and how he will respond. For instance, if a character is faced with hardships, the way in which he deals with them will define who he is. That is why setting and plot are important to character development. No story is complete without either one.

Read the excerpt:

> She had swum too far out. The waves were higher than she thought. She was struggling hard to get to shore. She wondered if she would make it. She thought of her childhood. Had she been right to run away from home, she wondered? Just then, a lifeguard grabbed her and helped her to shore.

How the setting influences the character in this excerpt.

The setting of the ocean and the high waves creates a conflict in the character. She is worried. She thinks about her childhood and her parents. She doesn't know if she will make it to shore. This is how the setting affects the character in this excerpt. Without the high waves and the struggle, she would not become so worried and start to think about her past. She probably would not have questioned herself. This is an example of how a setting influences a character. If the waves had not been high, there probably would not have been a struggle or any self-searching of the swimmer's past.

Figurative use of a word or expression

Figurative language is a literary device. Figurative language allows the author to expand reality in a vivid way. When an author uses figurative language, she connects things in an exaggerated way in order to create a memorable image. Examples of figurative language are: simile; metaphor, personification, and hyperbole. Similes compare things using the comparing words *like* or *as,* for example, "Don swims like a dolphin." Metaphors compare things without using comparing words—for example, "Don is a dolphin in the water." Personification gives a thing or animal human traits—for example, "The water welcomed Don back." Hyperbole is an exaggeration that is not believable—for example, "Don swims a million laps in the pool every morning."

Read the excerpt from the poem.

Roof-tops, roof-tops, what do you cover?

Sad folk, bad folk, and many a glowing lover;

Wise people, simple people, children of despair –

Roof-tops, roof-tops, hiding pain and care.

From "City Roofs" by Charles Hanson Towne

Tell what form of figurative language this is an example of and why.

This is an example of personification. In the poem, the poet asks the roof-tops, "what do you cover?" The poet is talking to the roof-tops as though they were people. In the excerpt, the roof-tops are treated like people; they are given human traits. This is the definition of what personification is. It is not an example of simile; there is no comparison using the words "as" or "like." It is not metaphor either because there is no comparison between two things sharing a similar quality. It is not an example of hyperbole; there is no exaggeration.

Difference between the denotative and connotative meaning of words

The denotative meaning of a word is the exact dictionary definition of the word. The connotative meaning of a word is what the word suggests. It is the emotion that is conveyed by the use of the word in context. The word may have associated meaning in addition to its dictionary definition. For example, the word "economical" is defined in the dictionary as saving money. But when the word is changed to "cheap" it takes on a different meaning, a more negative meaning. On the other hand, another synonym might be "frugal," which has a more positive meaning. Connotations are a subjective understanding of words. In such cases, the connotative meaning of a word in a passage can be found by looking at the context clues in the surrounding sentences.

Read the following sentence.

The outfit that Danae was wearing was not only attractive, it was stunning.

Explain the connotative meanings of the word "stunning" and how it relates to the word "attractive."

Both words, "stunning" and "attractive," mean "good looking." But the word "stunning" means that something is extremely good looking, so good looking as to catch someone's eye or stun a person. This word expresses a superlative rather than the word "attractive," which is less emphatic. Many things are attractive, but few are stunning. It is important to pick words that fit the situation, as this sentence does. Another word that means attractive is "cute," but as you can see, the connotations of this word are very different from "stunning." "Cute" means nice or pleasant, but it does not mean stunning, and yet both words mean attractive.

Impact of rhyme and other repetitions of sounds on literature

Sound elements play with the way words sound. They are common in poetry and in spoken forms of writing like speeches and plays. For example, rhyme repeats the ending sound: "So very soon/We will fly to the moon" and is frequently used in poetry, mostly older forms of poetry rather than modern poems. Alliteration repeats beginning sounds, usually consonants: "Rah, rah, rah," the crowd cried, "rah, rah, rah." It is often used in spoken forms of writing as well as in poetry. Onomatopoeia uses a word that sounds like what it is: "Bees go buzz, buzz, buzz and snakes go hiss, hiss." It is often used in poetry for children.

Explain the rhyme scheme of the following excerpt from a poem by Edgar Allan Poe.

Alone - Edgar Allan Poe

From childhood's hour I have not been
As others were; I have not seen
As others saw; I could not bring
My passions from a common spring.
From the same source I have not taken
My sorrow; I could not awaken
My heart to joy at the same tone;
And all I loved, I loved alone.

The rhyme scheme that Edgar Allan Poe uses in this excerpt from his poem "Alone" is: a, a; b, b, c, c, d, d, e, e. Every two lines rhyme but the rhyme is not repeated in the other lines. This is a rather unusual rhyme scheme; many others have lines that repeat the rhyme scheme, but not in a consecutive order, such as a, b, a, b or a, b, c a, b, c. Rhymes are at the discretion of the poet, and are

- 118 -

not mandatory. Many modern poems—actually, most of them—use a blank verse, where there are no rhyme schemes. There are many formal poetic types, such as the sonnet, that have a specific rhyme scheme that poets must follow to achieve that kind of poetic form.

Soliloquy

Soliloquies play a large role in shaping a play or drama because they allow the audience to have first-hand knowledge of what a character is feeling or thinking without having the interference of the other characters in the play. Soliloquies are really moments of the character being one on one with the audience. They are a chance for a character to bare his or her soul to the world in general. This experience creates an intensity of feeling between the character and the audience that leads to greater understanding of the character's personal plight and the meaning of the play. Such famous soliloquies as "To be or not to be" by Hamlet in the Shakespearean play of the same name live on because of the way in which they capture a human need to express doubt and a philosophy of life.

Poetic form of a sonnet impacts the meaning of poetry

The sonnet is an important poetic form because it is a brief experience of what a poet is feeling or perceiving about life. Sonnets differ from other forms of poetry, such as odes or narrative poetry, because of these characteristics. The sonnet has a long history and was developed in Italy and then adapted by the British. Consequently, there are various forms of sonnets, but all sonnets have strict guidelines in terms of length and rhyme scheme. Sonnets are seen both as a challenge and as fundamental to poetry because of their brevity and lucidity. Shakespeare's sonnets are extremely famous and give a face to the playwright because they are so very personal. Most great poets have at one time or another used the sonnet for an expression of themselves and their lives.

Drama or poem's form contributes to its meaning

The form or structure of a drama or poem is extremely important to the meaning of the text. There are many choices to be made when it comes to either form. Both poetry and drama come out of guidelines that were developed in Europe and England and then were brought to the United States, where they were used and sometimes changed to serve a different purpose. For instance, classically, the structure of a tragedy calls for a tragic or sad ending to the main character while a comedy never ends badly. However, both structures have been changed to meet the needs of modern society, and so today there are tragicomedies or comedic tragedies. The same is true of poetry. Strict rhyming poetry has given way to blank verse, for instance. And the choice of the structure of the poem or play gives the reader a hint as to its meaning.

Developing and contrasting the points of view of different characters or narrators in a text

An author uses many writing skills to develop a character's point of view in a piece of literature. By having a character respond to an event in a particular way, an author can show what the character thinks about it. Similarly, an author can choose to display a character's viewpoint through dialogue or actions. Various characters will have differing viewpoints and these can be shown in the conflict in a story or drama or even in a poem. Authors often display the narrator's point of view about characters, events, or the plot of a literary piece. The manner in which the author does this may be subtle or it may be overt. It is important to observe the language of the author, in order to analyze the author's and narrator's viewpoints about a character, an event, or a topic.

Read the following excerpt.

Clarisse went to the window. She looked out. As was her habit, she dismissed the entire scene. To her it was no more than two people showing off. She failed to notice the severity of the matter, nor could she foresee the outcome of this untimely fight.

Analyze the narrator's viewpoint of Clarisse.

The narrator seems to have a rather dim view of Clarisse. She says that Clarisse dismissed the "entire scene" of the two people who were outside her window showing off. This seems to suggest that the narrator thinks she doesn't really relate to what is going on. The narrator also says that Clarisse "failed to notice the severity of the matter," which also suggests that Clarisse doesn't have a deep understanding of what is happening. From these comments, the reader can figure out that the narrator is not praising Clarisse, but instead is somewhat critical of Clarisse. When determining a narrator's viewpoint of a character, be sure to watch for clues that tell you the narrator's opinion, such as the clues in this excerpt.

Effects on a written piece of literature when it is transformed into a film or multimedia version of itself

Modern films and multimedia versions of plays or other forms of fiction are indeed transformations of original pieces of literature. There are many parameters that will change the feeling, intent, intensity, and importance of the original work. They include the many technological advances that films and multimedia permit producers of such works. Many people read a book and then, when they see a movie based on it, are either happy with the outcome or upset. Lighting, sound, camera angles, whether or not the plot is followed closely, all affect the finished piece. While a balance between the original text and the move is preferable, this does not always occur because some producers prefer to use all that is available technologically, which may or may not prove fruitful. Certainly, the interpretation of a piece of literature to film or video is something that must be considered on many levels.

Historical fiction may or may not mirror reality

Historical fiction often deviates from the historical reality in order to tell a story and make the historical event more moving to the audience. Historical fiction, while being accurate for the most part, may take poetic license when it comes to individual characters or the details of a situation. For instance, a story might take place during the American Revolution. While the author would most certainly have the details of when and where an event took place, the author might fictionalize a character that was not mentioned in the actual accounts of the battle. Or the author could take a person who was mentioned and turn this person into a character of his or her liking. When reading historical fiction, you need always remind yourself that all the details mentioned are not accurate; this is why it is called historical fiction rather than history.

Read the following soliloquy.

> *Time was that I was young, but now I am old and grey. No one sees me. No one hears me. It is age that they see, only age. This is my life for now. My youth is gone.*

How does this soliloquy contribute to the meaning of a text or drama?

It explains how the character feels about growing old. It shows the inner thoughts of the character and what the character feels about himself. The speaker obviously does not like being old. The speaker thinks that he is no longer seen by the people around him. In other words the speaker feels useless to a large degree. The speech is also a commentary about society, that youth is the only force that is viable and that old age is not able to achieve anything that is meaningful. This is how the soliloquy would affect a text or drama.

Analyze the feelings in the excerpt of this sonnet by William Shakespeare.

> How do I love thee? Let me count the ways.
>
> I love thee to the depth and breadth and height
>
> My soul can reach, when feeling out of sight
>
> For the ends of Being and ideal Grace.

The poet is expressing his love for someone, and he uses language that shows that he loves the person very much. He loves to the depth, breadth, and height of his soul. This is very common in the sonnet form. It is often used to express the feelings of the poet. Sonnets are a form of poetry that many poets have used. Sonnets have very strict rhyme patterns and follow other guidelines. But they do allow the poet to express his or her own feelings, unlike other kinds of poems.

Describe the interaction between Melissa and Sam in the following passage.

> Melissa read Sam's report. She rolled her eyes. "You have no idea how to do this, do you?" Sam looked crestfallen.

The interaction between Melissa and Sam is that Melissa is criticizing Sam's report and Sam is upset by what she says. You can tell this from what Melissa says to Sam and the description of how Sam looks as he reacts to her words. It is important to analyze any reaction between people, events, or ideas when reading a passage. Besides fiction, there is a great deal of interaction between individuals, events, and ideas in an informational text. For instance, a persuasive passage will doubtless affect the reader because of the stance it takes on a particular subject. What the author says will have a reaction, whether it is positive or negative. There are interactions in other kinds of nonfiction as well. A text that covers a particular person or event will elicit feelings about what has been stated. For instance, in newspaper articles, people learn about people who have done newsworthy acts; they also read about events that are historic.

Informational Texts

Inference

Explicit information is information that is stated in a passage. It is stated right in the text; it is not suggested or hinted at. Explicit information can be facts or details about a topic. Frequently this information supports a main idea or thesis. Explicit information can be found just by reading a text, especially an informational passage. The explicit information in passages can, however, be used to form the basis for an inference. When making an inference, you need to put together the explicit information to form a conclusion. It is the best guess that a reader can make based on the information given in a passage.

Read the following excerpt. Tell whether it contains explicit information or not.

> I think the most famous person in the Old West is Annie Oakley. Annie is the best rifle shot who ever lived. She almost never missed. Many men challenged her to contests of speed and accuracy. She won them all.

Most of the information in the excerpt is explicit information. The information tells the reader about Annie Oakley: that she was the best rifle shot who ever lived and that she almost never missed. It also says that many men challenged her to contests and she won them all. This information is found right in the excerpt. It is not suggested or hinted at. Everything that is said is clearly what it means. The first sentence is a personal opinion; it is also explicit because the reader does not have to guess what the author thinks of Annie Oakley.

Read the passage.

> The Vikings set out in their boats in summer. The number of people in Scandinavia was growing fast. They needed to grow more food. In the late 900s, Eric the Red sailed across the Atlantic to Greenland. In 985, Viking farmers settled in Greenland.

Discuss why the conclusion that the Vikings were searching for new farmland is valid.

When you make an inference, you need to look at the information in the passage. The passage says that the Viking population was growing and that they needed to be able to grow more food. It is logical to guess that they sailed in search of new farmland. There is really not another possibility. Remember, inferences are assumptions that are hinted at or suggested by the text. They are not like explicit information; they are implicit in the text based on the explicit information that is found there. They are the best guess a reader can make.

Determining the main ideas of a passage

Main ideas are what passages are mostly about. They are the important ideas that a reader comes away with after reading a passage. It is why the passage is written. Passages may have more than one main idea; paragraphs may have a main idea of their own, or the entire passage could have more than one main idea. What determines a main idea is that it is the far-reaching thought that the passage or paragraph is about. It is not a detail. Details in a passage or paragraph may support the main idea, that is, they tell more about the main idea, but they are not the main idea.

Decide what the main idea is of the passage that follows and why it is the main idea.

> You can save yourself a lot of money if you learn how to refinish furniture. When you refinish a piece of furniture, you get rid of all the marks and scratches that have accumulated over the years. Your furniture looks like new. You can also give it a different look by changing the color of the stain, paint, or varnish.

The main idea is that refinishing is a good way to improve old furniture. The author tells us ways that refinishing can improve old furniture. This is the main idea of the passage. Everything else in the passage is a supporting detail. Always make sure that when figuring out the main idea of a passage, you choose what the passage is mostly about, not what one section is about or something about the main idea. This passage is short, so there is only one main idea in it. When analyzing which statement is a main idea, make sure to choose one that has a broad message, not one that is talking about something specific.

Determining the meaning of words and phrases from the way they are used in a text

The meanings of words and phrases can be determined from the way they are used in a text by using the context clues that are available in a passage. For instance, in the following sentences, there are context clues that help the reader understand the meaning of "cordial."

The salesperson smiled when the couple came into the store. She told them to take their time in choosing a ring. She chatted with them about their future plans. She was the most *cordial* salesperson they had ever met.

From these sentences, the reader can figure out that the meaning of cordial is friendly. The salesperson smiled; she told them to take their time; she chatted with them. She was friendly. These are context clues that help the reader figure out the meaning of a word. The same can be done with phrases.

Read the sentence and explain the meaning of "sense of foreboding."

All day long Ron kept thinking about Sue. For some unknown reason he was worried about her. He had a strong *sense of foreboding* that something was about to go wrong in Sue's city. Then he heard about the earthquake there. Luckily Sue was not injured.

To figure out the meaning of the phrase "sense of foreboding," the reader needs to look for context clues in just the same way the reader would do to figure out the meaning of a single word. The excerpt says that Ron was "worried" about Sue for "some unknown reason." It also says that he felt that "something was going to go wrong in Sue's city." Ron also heard about an earthquake taking place in Sue's city. A "sense of foreboding" must mean that Ron had an idea that something bad was going to happen. The context clues help the reader figure out the meaning of the phrase.

Read the excerpt below and, using context clues, decide what the word "disbursed" means.

It was May and Francesca hadn't received her insurance money. She wondered why it was taking so long. She needed the money to pay the contractor. When she called, a woman said that the money would be *disbursed* soon. That made Francesca feel better.

Using context clues is a good way to figure out the meanings of words and expressions without having to look them up in the dictionary. The way to discover context clues is to study the text. The excerpt says that Francesca had not received her insurance money for the hurricane's damage. It says that she had done the paperwork and that she needed the money to pay for the repair work to the house. Francesca felt a lot better when a woman at the insurance office said it would be disbursed by June 1. If you substitute the word "sent" for "disbursed," you can see that it makes sense. It fits with all the context clues and explains why Francesca would feel better.

Figurative language

Authors often make use of figurative language, which allows the writer to expand the way in which he or she uses language. Figurative language uses words in a non-literal way; this means that the word or expression takes on a new meaning. For instance, an author might say that Tom is like a robot. While everyone knows that Tom is a person, the image of Tom as a robot casts a new means of description. Figurative language takes many forms; it can be in the form of a simile, a metaphor, personification, or hyperbole. Similes compare things using the comparing word *like* or *as*—for example, "Tom is like a robot." Metaphors compare things without using comparing words—for example, "Tom is a robot when it comes to numbers." Personification gives a thing or animal human traits—for example, "The machine beckoned to Tom."

Read the excerpt written by Martin Luther King, Jr.

"One hundred years later, the Negro is still languishing in the corners of American society and finds himself an exile in his own land."

Discuss what King means when he calls the Negro "an exile in his own land."

Dr. King uses metaphors to express what he feels about the plight of the American Negro in this excerpt, especially in the metaphor where he likens the Negro to an exile in his own land. An exile is someone who is cast out, but in this case he is in his own land, so this is extremely sad and a very effective way of demonstrating the problems that African Americans were facing. Figurative language is a strong and effective way to get a point across, as in the case of this metaphor. Such a metaphor makes people sit up and listen to what is being said.

Connotations of the word "ragged" as compared with the expression "worn out"

The word "ragged" and the expression "worn out" both mean old and used, but "ragged" suggests something stronger. It suggests that the object is "in rags" and looking terrible; "worn out" merely means that something is old and used, but it does not suggest that it is in rags or terrible looking. Connotations carry many secondary meanings, so it is important to choose words that fit the situation. They are also filled with emotional meanings that should be analyzed and understood before choosing the word that you want to use. A dress may look worn out, but that dress probably does not look ragged. There is a difference in meaning, so it is important for the writer to choose the most accurate word.

Determining the structure that an author uses in a passage

There are basically seven different kinds of structures that are used in passages: question and answer order, chronological or sequential order, problem and solution order, cause and effect order, compare and contrast order, order of importance, and spatial order. There are often combinations of these structures in longer passages. Question and answer order opens with a question and then gives the answer; chronological order gives events in the order that they happen; problem and solution order offers a problem and then resolves it; cause and effect has a cause that results in a certain effect; compare and contrast is used to compare two ideas, things, or people; order of importance is self-explanatory; and spatial order is where a passage is ordered according to how something looks or where things are located.

Tom is doing a report on good nutrition and what the benefits of eating right are. He is beginning to write his essay. Describe which type of order would probably work best for his report and why.

The best choice would probably be a cause and effect organization for the report. A cause and effect order would allow the author to list the benefit of healthy eating and the effects of not eating well so that they would be easily comprehended by the reader. A compare and contrast order might also be considered, but if the emphasis is on the benefits of healthful eating, a cause and effect order would be more to the point and more effective. Obviously, a chronological order would have no place in the report, nor would a spatial order. The order an author uses is usually central to the topic the author chooses.

Determining an author's point of view

The author's point of view may be clear or it may be hidden. It is important to read a text closely to find out exactly what the author thinks about the event, person, topic, or issue that the author is writing about. When reading, look for clues to the author's viewpoint in terms of emotional statements or critiques of others discussing the topic. Some authors make their viewpoints very clear by stating it at the beginning of a text; but others want to keep their own opinions somewhat secret for many possible reasons. The author may not want to appear biased in one way or another and certainly some authors try very hard to stay objective. Still there are other authors who have a definite viewpoint but choose to conceal it and use other writers' comments to convey their own viewpoint. The reason it is important to ascertain an author's viewpoint is to ensure that you are reading something that gives a total picture of the topic, without bias.

Read the following excerpt:

> Dear Editor: We must support the "Save-the-Buffalo" bill before Congress. Anyone with any concern about animal life and the environment must support this bill. The people who vote against it are selfish fools who don't care about the environment.

Describe the viewpoint of the author and tell if the letter could be improved.

The author of the letter's viewpoint is clear; he states what he thinks right away. He is in favor of the "Save-the-Buffalo" bill and he argues that people should support it if they care about the environment. He also insults those who are against by the bill by calling them selfish fools and saying they don't care about the environment. This letter is not subtle in any way. It is the complete opposite. The letter could be improved by the author using facts or figures to back up his argument rather than insulting those who do not agree with him.

Explain the purpose of the passage below:

> The gray whale is a baleen whale; it has no teeth. Instead it has sieve-like plates that hang from the upper jaw to filter krill, plankton, and other small organisms from the sea water. The baleen plates are always wearing out and continue to grow throughout the whale's life.

This passage talks about baleen whales and gives details about them. There is nothing in the passage that tries to persuade the reader and there are no statements of opinion in the passage at all. Instead all of the statements are facts. This is what a passage does that has as its purpose to inform. It states details or facts about a topic. This passage is not funny, so it is not meant to amuse. The passage does not solve any problem, request anything, or narrate a story either. That is how the reader can tell that its purpose is to inform.

Oral delivery of a text will affect its impact on a listener

The written word becomes a completely different tool when it is spoken. Depending on the tone of the speaker, words take on new life and those that seemed to be benign may become strong statements that will propel the listener into action. Audio texts help listeners to hear the tone and intent of a speaker, but videos have an even greater impact because seeing a person speak is even more energizing (or not) than simply listening. The demeanor of the speaker can be analyzed and it will affect the way someone listening responds to a text. Consequently, multimedia versions are even more effective because they can add music, videos, or whatever effects a producer wishes to include. The multimedia versions of a text can have far-reaching effects, probably much more powerful than ever envisioned by the author of the text itself.

Assessing whether an argument in a text is sound and valid

When reading a persuasive text, it is important to analyze whether an argument is sound and valid and also whether the evidence that is given to support the argument is relevant and sufficient to support a claim. For instance, make sure to understand and research the topic of the passage and the opinions that the author is offering. Look at the supporting evidence and notice where it comes from. Is the evidence filled with opinions or is it based on facts? Are the facts from a source that is reliable or from a source that cannot be substantiated? Beware of claims that try to make a connection on an emotional level or arguments that tug at possible biases or prejudices. Make sure to reread the material more than once before taking any of the arguments or evidence seriously.

Analyzing the works of two or more authors on the same topic

When reading about a single topic that has been the subject of two or more texts, there are several things that must be done to compare them objectively. The reader needs to read each text carefully and take note of the point of view of the author as well as the reason the work was written. For instance, one author may be writing an opinion piece about a person and the person's beliefs, while a second writer may be doing an analysis of what the person has done and the kinds of issues the person is involved in. These two approaches could work to help the reader learn a great deal about a subject, from both a subjective and an objective manner. Another author might choose to write a biography about the same subject, which would lend more of an understanding of the person's life and those things that influenced her. When reading multiple texts about a single subject, it is wise to keep notes so that you can refer back and see the various ways in which one topic is presented. Reading more than one text on a subject certainly is a broadening experience.

Practice Test

Practice Questions

Questions 1 – 4 are based on the following:

The Blue and the Gray

by Francis Miles Finch

By the flow of the inland river,

    Whence the fleets of iron have fled,

Where the blades of the grave-grass quiver,

    Asleep are the ranks of the dead:

      Under the sod and the dew,

        Waiting the judgment-day;

      Under the one, the Blue,

        Under the other, the Gray

These in the robings of glory,

    Those in the gloom of defeat,

All with the battle-blood gory,

    In the dusk of eternity meet:

      Under the sod and the dew,

        Waiting the judgment-day

      Under the laurel, the Blue,

        Under the willow, the Gray.

From the silence of sorrowful hours

    The desolate mourners go,

Lovingly laden with flowers

    Alike for the friend and the foe;

      Under the sod and the dew,

        Waiting the judgment-day;

Under the roses, the Blue,

    Under the lilies, the Gray.

So with an equal splendor,

    The morning sun-rays fall,

With a touch impartially tender,

    On the blossoms blooming for all:

    Under the sod and the dew,

      Waiting the judgment-day;

    Broidered with gold, the Blue,

      Mellowed with gold, the Gray.

So, when the summer calleth,

    On forest and field of grain,

With an equal murmur falleth

    The cooling drip of the rain:

    Under the sod and the dew,

      Waiting the judgment-day,

    Wet with the rain, the Blue

    Wet with the rain, the Gray.

Sadly, but not with upbraiding,

    The generous deed was done,

In the storm of the years that are fading

    No braver battle was won:

    Under the sod and the dew,

      Waiting the judgment-day;

    Under the blossoms, the Blue,

      Under the garlands, the Gray

No more shall the war cry sever,

    Or the winding rivers be red;

They banish our anger forever

When they laurel the graves of our dead!

Under the sod and the dew,

Waiting the judgment-day,

Love and tears for the Blue,

Tears and love for the Gray.

1. What type of scene does this poem depict?
   a. the changing of the seasons
   b. a loved one being welcomed home
   c. the aftermath of a battle
   d. a decision being made

2. What do the following lines imply about those who died as a result of the actions that were taken?

Love and tears for the Blue,

Tears and love for the Gray.

   a. Those who died in battle are now weeping as a result of their destruction.
   b. It doesn't matter who won the battle; there are people on both sides mourning their loved ones.
   c. Bystanders are questioning the reasons for the battle that took so many lives.
   d. One day, those who died will come back to life.

3. How does the author's repetition of the idea expressed in the following lines help communicate his main message?

Under the sod and the dew,

Waiting the judgment-day,

Love and tears for the Blue,

Tears and love for the Gray.

   a. It shows that there are no winners when it comes to war, only destruction, and that in death, everyone is equal.
   b. It tells the reader that battles should be remembered and reenacted to remember the losses once suffered.
   c. It shows that those who die in battle should never be remembered for their sacrifices.
   d. It reminds readers that it is not their job to wonder at the reasons behind war, but to follow the actions of others and mourn losses when they happen.

4. The author contrasts images of death and destruction with those of natural beauty and wonder to show that

   a. war is pointless.
   b. there are just reasons for war and violence.
   c. even in the aftermath of horrific violence, life continues to go on and renew itself.
   d. we should be thankful for what we have today and not worry about what we will need in the future.

Questions 5– 8 are based on the following:

The following is an excerpt from Anne of Green Gables, *a classic story written by Lucy Maud Montgomery that follows the life and times of a young girl who was mistakenly sent to live with an elderly brother and sister in rural Prince Edward Island.*

Morning at Green Gables

It was broad daylight when Anne awoke and sat up in bed, staring confusedly at the window through which a flood of cheery sunshine was pouring and outside of which something white and feathery waved across glimpses of blue sky.

For a moment she could not remember where she was. First came a delightful thrill, as something very pleasant; then a horrible remembrance. This was Green Gables and they didn't want her because she wasn't a boy!

But it was morning and, yes, it was a cherry-tree in full bloom outside of her window. With a bound she was out of bed and across the floor. She pushed up the sash—it went up stiffly and creakily, as if it hadn't been opened for a long time, which was the case; and it stuck so tight that nothing was needed to hold it up.

Anne dropped on her knees and gazed out into the June morning, her eyes glistening with delight. Oh, wasn't it beautiful? Wasn't it a lovely place? Suppose she wasn't really going to stay here! She would imagine she was. There was scope for imagination here.

A huge cherry-tree grew outside, so close that its boughs tapped against the house, and it was so thick-set with blossoms that hardly a leaf was to be seen. On both sides of the house were a big orchard, one of apple-trees and one of cherry-trees, also showered over with blossoms; and their grass was all sprinkled with dandelions. In the garden below were lilac-trees purple with flowers, and their dizzily sweet fragrance drifted up to the window on the morning wind.

Below the garden a green field lush with clover sloped down to the hollow where the brook ran and where scores of white birches grew, upspringing airily out of an undergrowth suggestive of delightful possibilities in ferns and mosses and woodsy things generally. Beyond it was a hill, green and feathery with spruce and fir; there was a gap in it where the gray gable end of the little house she had seen from the other side of the Lake of Shining Waters was visible.

Off to the left were the big barns and beyond them, away down over green, low-sloping fields, was a sparkling blue glimpse of sea.

- 130 -

Anne's beauty-loving eyes lingered on it all, taking everything greedily in. She had looked on so many unlovely places in her life, poor child; but this was as lovely as anything she had ever dreamed.

She knelt there, lost to everything but the loveliness around her, until she was startled by a hand on her shoulder. Marilla had come in unheard by the small dreamer.

"It's time you were dressed," she said curtly.

Marilla really did not know how to talk to the child, and her uncomfortable ignorance made her crisp and curt when she did not mean to be.

Anne stood up and drew a long breath.

"Oh, isn't it wonderful?" she said, waving her hand comprehensively at the good world outside.

"It's a big tree," said Marilla, "and it blooms great, but the fruit don't amount to much never—small and wormy."

"Oh, I don't mean just the tree; of course it's lovely—yes, it's RADIANTLY lovely—it blooms as if it meant it—but I meant everything, the garden and the orchard and the brook and the woods, the whole big dear world. Don't you feel as if you just loved the world on a morning like this? And I can hear the brook laughing all the way up here. Have you ever noticed what cheerful things brooks are? They're always laughing. Even in winter-time I've heard them under the ice. I'm so glad there's a brook near Green Gables. Perhaps you think it doesn't make any difference to me when you're not going to keep me, but it does. I shall always like to remember that there is a brook at Green Gables even if I never see it again. If there wasn't a brook I'd be HAUNTED by the uncomfortable feeling that there ought to be one. I'm not in the depths of despair this morning. I never can be in the morning. Isn't it a splendid thing that there are mornings? But I feel very sad. I've just been imagining that it was really me you wanted after all and that I was to stay here forever and ever. It was a great comfort while it lasted. But the worst of imagining things is that the time comes when you have to stop and that hurts."

"You'd better get dressed and come down-stairs and never mind your imaginings," said Marilla as soon as she could get a word in edgewise. "Breakfast is waiting. Wash your face and comb your hair. Leave the window up and turn your bedclothes back over the foot of the bed. Be as smart as you can."

This question has two parts. Answer part A, then answer part B.

5. Part A: Which words best describe how Anne is feeling?
    a. shy and inactive
    b. scared and unsure of her situation
    c. energized and excited about the possibility that Green Gables will be her new home
    d. excited, but a little homesick for the orphanage

Part B: Give a sentence from the passage that supports your answer in Part A.

_____

_____

_____

This question has two parts. Answer part A, then answer part B.

6. Part A: The word <u>smart</u> as used in the final line of the passage means
   a. quick
   b. intelligent
   c. painful
   d. fashionable

Part B: Which word is the best synonym for <u>smart</u> based on your answer from Part A.
   a. swift
   b. tidy
   c. fancy
   d. intelligent

7. Which of the following describes how Marilla feels about Anne?
   a. Marilla has decided that she does not like Anne, and will send her back to the orphanage.
   b. Marilla is warming up to Anne and starting to feel affection for her.
   c. Marilla is unsure of how to act around Anne, and is uncomfortable with a child in the house.
   d. Marilla is suspicious of Anne and of whether her being sent to Green Gables was really a mistake.

8. What is the author's purpose in presenting the following as Anne's response to Marilla's misunderstanding of Anne gesturing out the window?

> *"Oh, I don't mean just the tree; of course it's lovely—yes, it's RADIANTLY lovely—it blooms as if it meant it—but I meant everything, the garden and the orchard and the brook and the woods, the whole big dear world. Don't you feel as if you just loved the world on a morning like this? And I can hear the brook laughing all the way up here. Have you ever noticed what cheerful things brooks are? They're always laughing. Even in winter-time I've heard them under the ice. I'm so glad there's a brook near Green Gables. Perhaps you think it doesn't make any difference to me when you're not going to keep me, but it does. I shall always like to remember that there is a brook at Green Gables even if I never see it again. If there wasn't a brook I'd be HAUNTED by the uncomfortable feeling that there ought to be one. I'm not in the depths of despair this morning. I never can be in the morning. Isn't it a splendid thing that there are mornings? But I feel very sad. I've just been imagining that it was really me you wanted after all and that I was to stay here for ever and ever. It was a great comfort while it lasted. But the worst of imagining things is that the time comes when you have to stop and that hurts."*

a. to show Anne's tendency for being dramatic and establish an important component of her personality

b. to show Anne's fear that Marilla misunderstood her intentions when she was gesturing out the window

c. to correct a misperception and prevent Marilla from being angry with Anne

d. to show Marilla the extent of Anne's intelligence in the hopes that she will not be sent back to the orphanage

Questions 9 – 13 are based on the following:

The following is an excerpt of an article published by The New York Times *announcing the assassination of President Abraham Lincoln.*

AWFUL EVENT

President Lincoln Shot by an Assassin

The Deed Done at Ford's Theatre Last Night

THE ACT OF A DESPERATE REBEL

The President Still Alive at Last Accounts

No Hopes Entertained of His Recovery

Attempted Assassination of Secretary Seward

DETAILS OF THE DREADFUL TRAGEDY.

Official

War Department, Washington April 15, 1:30 A.M. - Maj. Gen. Dis.: This evening at about 9:30 P.M. at Ford's Theatre, the President, while sitting in his private box with Mrs. Lincoln, Mr. Harris, and Major Rathburn, was shot by an assassin, who suddenly entered the box and appeared behind the President.

The assassin then leaped upon the stage, brandishing a large dagger or knife, and made his escape in the rear of the theatre.

The pistol ball entered the back of the President's head and penetrated nearly through the head. The wound is <u>mortal</u>. The President has been insensible ever since it was inflicted, and is now dying.

About the same hour an assassin, whether the same or not, entered Mr. Sewards' apartments, and under the pretense of having a prescription, was shown to the Secretary's sick chamber. The assassin immediately rushed to the bed, and inflicted two or three stabs on the throat and two on the face. It is hoped the wounds may not be mortal. My apprehension is that they will prove fatal.

The nurse alarmed Mr. Frederick Seward, who was in an adjoining room, and hastened to the door of his father's room, when he met the assassin, who inflicted upon him one or more dangerous wounds. The recovery of Frederick Seward is doubtful.

- 133 -

It is not probable that the President will live throughout the night.

Gen. Grant and wife were advertised to be at the theatre this evening, but he started to Burlington at 6 o'clock this evening.

At a Cabinet meeting at which Gen. Grant was present, the subject of the state of the country and the prospect of a speedy peace was discussed. The President was very cheerful and hopeful, and spoke very kindly of Gen. Lee and others of the Confederacy, and of the establishment of government in Virginia.

All the members of the Cabinet except Mr. Seward are now in attendance upon the President.

I have seen Mr. Seward, but he and Frederick were both unconscious.

Edwin M. Stanton, Secretary of War.

9. The underlined word <u>mortal</u> means
   a. recuperative.
   b. painful.
   c. fatal.
   d. risky.

10. What is a likely purpose for including so many headlines at the start of the article?
   a. to quickly convey the most important information about a significant event
   b. to sensationalize a front-page news story
   c. to incite panic in readers
   d. to fill empty space on the page

11. Who is the author of this article?
   a. The New York Times
   b. Edwin M. Stanton
   c. Frederick Seward
   d. Major Rathburn

12. Write a summary of the article.

_____

_____

_____

13. What is implied by the following sentence?
It is hoped the wounds may not be mortal. My apprehension is that they will prove fatal.

   a. Those involved with the events are hopeful for a positive outcome.
   b. There is no hope that Seward or Lincoln will recover from their wounds.
   c. The writer is pessimistic about whether Seward will recover from his wounds.
   d. The writer is doubtful about the legitimacy of accounts regarding the night's events.

Questions 14 – 18 are based on the following:

Carter's teacher asked him to write a short essay about whether or not everyone in America should vote. The following is the essay he wrote in response to this prompt from his seventh-grade social studies teacher.

(1) George Washington and all of the other great leaders who fought in the Revolutionary War would be very disappointed in Americans today. (2) The right to choose who will represent us in government has lost its importance. (3) Too many people do not vote in elections and are just throwing away their right our founding fathers fought to give them. (4) If people do not stand up and choose their own leaders, someone else will do it for them: and who knows what those leaders will stand for? (5) Many people struggled and died to give us the right to vote, and we should always honor that sacrifice by voting in every election.

(6) The main purpose of the Revolutionary War was to break free from rulers who did not give their people a say in their own government. (7) British colonists in America lived far away from their leaders in the British Parliament, and could not have a physical presence in government due to the distance between America and England. (8) This led to a denial of the rights that these colonists would have had if they still lived in England. (9) Tired of "taxation without representation," as the popular slogan went during this time in history, the colonists felt so strongly that they should have a say in their government that they took up arms against their own countrymen and fought for their freedom.

(10) Today, Americans take the fact that they have had voting rights for over 200 years for granted. (11) That's why voting isn't as important as it was back in the day. (12) If you look at how other people and countries have all fought for the right to vote, and continue to do so even today, it's plain to see that voting is something that should still be important in our society.

(13) We should all remember the sacrifices that have been made to ensure our freedoms, and we should take full advantage of those freedoms. (14) If we don't, those who died to ensure that all Americans have the right to life, liberty, and the pursuit of happiness will have died in vain. (15) I hope that my generation will be the first of many to make voting one of our most important and treasured rights once again.

14. Which of the following answer choices presents the best revision of sentence 3?

a. Too many people do not vote in elections and just throw away their right our founding fathers fought to give them.
b. Too many people do not vote in elections, and, as a result, throw away one of the basic rights our founding fathers fought so hard to ensure for future generations.
c. Too many people today do not value their right to vote as much as our founding fathers.
d. Too many people choose not to vote in elections and throw away our founding fathers' rights.

15. Which of the following is the best way to revise sentence 11 so that the style the writer uses throughout the rest of the essay is maintained?

    a. Our culture has devalued voting to the point that many simply do not care that an entire war was fought so that they could have that right in the first place.
    b. Voting isn't as important as it was back in the day.
    c. The devaluation of the right to vote by American society has resulted in the overall apathy of our citizenry when it comes to exercising the rights given to them as a result of the Revolutionary War.
    d. People don't think of voting as important anymore.

16. Which sentence, if added after sentence 10, would make Carter's point in the third paragraph more persuasive?

    a. The fights about voting rights that people in other countries are engaged in even now seem so far removed from life in the U.S.
    b. Americans don't have any memory of having to fight for the right to have a voice in government.
    c. For the most part, our citizens have had the right to vote for their entire lives; it's something that has just always been there.
    d. They should remember that this right was something that had to be fought for, not something that was given to all citizens.

17. Which sentence states the main point of Carter's essay?

    a. 2
    b. 3
    c. 4
    d. 5

18. Which of the following pieces of advice would you give Carter to help him make his argument clearer and more persuasive?

    a. Ask a few questions about why Americans today don't value their right to vote.
    b. Provide more information about how and why Americans today do not value their right to vote, including examples and statistics.
    c. Add in a personal story about your family's history as Revolutionary War activists.
    d. Provide more information about why the British colonists chose to fight for independence.

Questions 19 – 21 are based on the following:

Jordan was asked to look at the following image showing the American/Mexican border and write about what she sees and how she feels about it. The following is her response to this image.

(1) This picture makes me feel conflicted. (2) The United States is shown on the left side; Mexico is on the right. (3) In the middle is a thin fence that separates two entire countries. (4) It seems insignificant in comparison to the great nations that lay on both sides of the fence. (5) But, like the fence itself, this line has been made by people to define what piece of land belongs to whom. (6) And hasn't this very thing been the cause of wars throughout history?

(7) You can see the huge difference between the two sides of the border. (8) The U.S. side is full of open land. (9) There are only a few buildings and maybe a small settlement, and there are also more walls. (10) It's like this area of land is a cushion between the dividing line and the U.S. (11) On the other side, you can see that the Mexican settlement is very developed. (12) A major highway travels the length of the border only a few yards away from the fence itself. (13) There are a lot of houses, businesses, signs, and other closely-packed signs of life and activity that seem to be pushed as close to the fence as possible.

(14) This interpretation of the image makes me sad. (15) It's like the country of Mexico is eager to have a more active partnership with its neighboring country, but America doesn't want any part of it. (16) The fact that the Mexican side gets as close to the dividing line as possible while the American side has a buffer area shows this. (17) It's like the two countries are sharing a sandbox, and America doesn't want Mexico's sand coming anywhere near its sand. (18) On the other hand, I also feel hopeful that one day both sides will be able to come together and play nice, sharing their sand and toys instead of building fences.

- 137 -

19. The purpose of sentence 11 is to

    a. transition Jordan's discussion from details about the Mexican side of the border to details of the U.S. side of the border.
    b. transition Jordan's discussion from details about the U.S. side of the border to details of the Mexican side of the border.
    c. provide additional details to help the reader understand the content of the picture.
    d. provide an opinion about what the purpose of the picture is.

This question has two parts. Answer part A, then answer part B.

20. Part A: Which sentence shows Jordan's opinion about the picture?

    a. 12
    b. 14
    c. 15
    d. 17

Part B: Based on your answer in Part A, which of the following sentences supports Jordan's opinion of the image?

    a. 11
    b. 13
    c. 16
    d. 17

21. Jordan's comparison of the relationship between the U.S. and Mexico to children playing in a sandbox is an example of using

    a. a metaphor to better explain an abstract idea
    b. a simile to draw a comparison between an abstract idea and a concrete detail
    c. alliteration to emphasize a point
    d. none of the above

Questions 22– 25 are based on the following:

The following is an excerpt from The House of Mirth *by Edith Wharton. This novel tells the tragic tale of Lily Bart, a beautiful woman who lives the life of a socialite, even though she herself has no money, and must marry in order to maintain the lifestyle to which she has become accustomed. To do this, she must maintain her reputation as a desirable catch for wealthy suitors.*

In the hansom she leaned back with a sigh. Why must a girl pay so dearly for her least escape from routine? Why could one never do a natural thing without having to screen it behind a structure of artifice? She had yielded to a passing impulse in going to Lawrence Selden's rooms, and it was so seldom that she could allow herself the luxury of an impulse! This one, at any rate, was going to cost her rather more than she could afford. She was vexed to see that, in spite of so many years of vigilance, she had blundered twice within five minutes. That stupid story about her dress-maker was bad enough—it would have been so simple to tell Rosedale that she had been taking tea with Selden! The mere statement of the fact would have rendered it innocuous. But, after having let herself be surprised in a falsehood, it was doubly stupid to snub the witness of her discomfiture. If she had had the presence of mind to let Rosedale drive her to the station, the concession might have purchased his silence. He had his race's accuracy in the appraisal of values, and to be seen walking down the platform at the crowded afternoon hour in the company of Miss Lily Bart would have been money in his pocket, as he might himself have phrased it. He knew, of course, that there would be a large house-party at Bellomont, and the possibility of being taken for one of Mrs. Trenor's guests was doubtless included in his calculations. Mr. Rosedale was still at a stage in his social ascent when it was of importance to produce such impressions.

The provoking part was that Lily knew all this—knew how easy it would have been to silence him on the spot, and how difficult it might be to do so afterward. Mr. Simon Rosedale was a man who made it his business to know everything about every one, whose idea of showing himself to be at home in society was to display an inconvenient familiarity with the habits of those with whom he wished to be thought intimate. Lily was sure that within twenty-four hours the story of her visiting her dress-maker at the Benedick would be in active circulation among Mr. Rosedale's acquaintances. The worst of it was that she had always snubbed and ignored him. On his first appearance—when her improvident cousin, Jack Stepney, had obtained for him (in return for favours too easily guessed) a card to one of the vast impersonal Van Osburgh "crushes"—Rosedale, with that mixture of artistic sensibility and business astuteness which characterizes his race, had instantly gravitated toward Miss Bart. She understood his motives, for her own course was guided by as nice calculations. Training and experience had taught her to be hospitable to newcomers, since the most unpromising might be useful later on, and there were plenty of available oubliettes to swallow them if they were not. But some intuitive repugnance, getting the better of years of social discipline, had made her push Mr. Rosedale into his oubliette without a trial. He had left behind only the ripple of amusement which his speedy dispatch had caused among her friends; and though later (to shift the metaphor) he reappeared lower down the stream, it was only in fleeting glimpses, with long submergences between.

Hitherto Lily had been undisturbed by scruples. In her little set Mr. Rosedale had been pronounced "impossible," and Jack Stepney roundly snubbed for his attempt to pay his debts in dinner invitations. Even Mrs. Trenor, whose taste for variety had led her into some hazardous experiments, resisted Jack's attempts to disguise Mr. Rosedale as a novelty, and declared that he was the same little Jew who had been served up and rejected at the social board a dozen times within her memory; and while Judy Trenor was obdurate there was small chance of Mr. Rosedale's penetrating beyond the outer limbo of the Van Osburgh crushes. Jack gave up the contest with a laughing "You'll see," and, sticking manfully to his guns, showed himself with Rosedale at the fashionable restaurants, in company with the personally vivid if socially obscure ladies who are available for such purposes. But the attempt had hitherto been vain, and as Rosedale undoubtedly paid for the dinners, the laugh remained with his debtor.

Mr. Rosedale, it will be seen, was thus far not a factor to be feared—unless one put one's self in his power. And this was precisely what Miss Bart had done. Her clumsy fib had let him see that she had something to conceal; and she was sure he had a score to settle with her. Something in his smile told her he had not forgotten. She turned from the thought with a little shiver, but it hung on her all the way to the station, and dogged her down the platform with the persistency of Mr. Rosedale himself.

22. This passage is told from whose point of view?

    a. Simon Rosedale
    b. Lily Bart
    c. Jack Stepney
    d. Lawrence Selden

23. In the film version of *The House of Mirth*, this scene is portrayed by three actors. The audience observes Lily, Selden, and Rosedale meeting outside the Benedick, and watches the events that unfold. This change of medium makes analyzing the events through Lily's thoughts impossible, so much of the back story presented in the text is lost in the film version. What detail would most likely be missed by telling the story through the medium of film?

    a. Lily does not like Rosedale, but will keep up the pretenses of being sociable and polite to him in public.
    b. Lily is uncomfortable with the situation she is in.
    c. Lily lied about her reason for being at the Benedick.
    d. Rosedale has ulterior motives for offering Lily a ride.

24. What does "sticking manfully to his guns" mean as it is used in this passage?

    a. Jack Stepney could easily turn violent in the face of society's rejection of Rosedale.
    b. Rosedale is continuing to persist in his efforts to break into Lily's circle of friends, but is becoming discouraged by their constant rejection of him.
    c. Rosedale is optimistic that if he persists in his efforts to break into Lily's circle of friends, he will eventually be successful.
    d. Jack Stepney is standing behind his public support of Rosedale in important social circles, despite the fact that important members of society have snubbed them both for it.

25. References to Rosedale's "race" and lines such as "that he was the same little Jew who had been served up and rejected at the social board a dozen times within her memory" reveal what about Lily's set of friends?

    a. They are envious of Rosedale's success and charisma.
    b. They are afraid of Rosedale because of his family lineage.
    c. They are discriminating against Rosedale because he is Jewish.
    d. They are mistaken about where Rosedale's wealth came from.

Questions 26 – 29 are based on the following:

"The Gettysburg Address" was a speech given by President Abraham Lincoln on Nov. 19, 1863 at the dedication of the Gettysburg National Cemetery, the final resting place of soldiers killed in the Battle of Gettysburg during the Civil War.

The Gettysburg Address

Four score and seven years ago our fathers brought forth, upon this continent, a new nation, conceived in Liberty, and dedicated to the proposition that all men are created equal.

Now we are engaged in a great civil war, testing whether that nation, or any nation so conceived, and so dedicated, can long endure. We are met here on a great battlefield of that war. We have come to dedicate a portion of it as a final resting place for those who here gave their lives that that nation might live. It is altogether fitting and proper that we should do this.

But in a larger sense we cannot dedicate - we cannot consecrate - we cannot hallow this ground. The brave men, living and dead, who struggled here, have consecrated it far above our poor power to add or detract. The world will little note, nor long remember, what we say here, but can never forget what they did here.

It is for us, the living, rather to be dedicated here to the unfinished work which they have, thus far, so nobly carried on. It is rather for us to be here dedicated to the great task remaining before us - that from these honored dead we take increased devotion to that cause for which they here gave the last full measure of devotion - that we here highly resolve that these dead shall not have died in vain; that this nation shall have a new birth of freedom; and that this government of the people, by the people, for the people, shall not perish from the earth.

26. What is the main message of this speech?

a. Those who died in this battle honor this land we are dedicating today better than anyone else.
b. As we honor those who died in this battle, we should move forward with renewed dedication to ensuring the nation our founding fathers created continues to function the way they intended.
c. We need to put the regrets of the past aside, without remembering the sacrifices of those who gave their lives for our country.
d. The war we are fighting is far from over, as evidenced by the number of lives lost in this battle.

27. The phrase "the world will little note" means what?

a. The world will not soon forget.
b. The world will record what we say here.
c. The world will not pay much attention.
d. The world will recall what we do with perfect accuracy.

28. Why does Lincoln most likely talk about the past before he talks about the present?

a. to incite listeners of his message to protest
b. to remember what has been lost in the past
c. to establish context for his main message
d. to try to get listeners to side with his position

29. What is the following sentence addressing?

Now we are engaged in a great civil war, testing whether that nation, or any nation so conceived, and so dedicated, can long endure.

a. whether or not a nation based on ideas of freedom and equality can survive for any significant length of time
b. whether or not the Union will be able to preserve the existing structure of the United States by preventing the Confederacy from seceding
c. whether or not the Confederacy will be successful in seceding from the United States and surviving on its own
d. whether or not Lincoln should continue dedicating troops to the war

Answers and Explanations

1. C: There are many lines in this poem that indicate it is describing a scene following a battle: By the flow of the inland river / Whence the fleets of iron have fled; These in the robings of glory / Those in the gloom of defeat / All with the battle-blood gory / In the dusk of eternity meet; and No braver battle was won. Each of these lines implies that some kind of battle took place, but is now over.

2. B: These lines use the same words to describe the emotions of those on both sides of the conflict. The only difference is the order of the words, which does not affect their meaning in any way. This author is saying that there are tears and love for all of the people who lost their lives as a result of this battle. There is no indication that this is the view of the dead, or that, if indeed there are bystanders present in this section of the poem, they are questioning anything. There is also no indication that the dead will come back to life.

3. A: These lines can be interpreted to mean that soldiers from both sides of the battle now lay dead and buried, and face the same fate. No matter the circumstances depicted in the lines preceding these in each stanza, the dead still lie beneath the soil awaiting the afterlife. This makes death an equalizer. The fact that this is repeated over and over in the poem shows its significance.

4. C: The author begins the poem with images of ending and destruction, such as *in the gloom of defeat* and *All with the battle-blood gory / In the dusk of eternity meet.* Then, he transitions into a blending of these images with ones such as *the morning sun-rays fall* and *a touch impartially tender / On the blossoms blooming for all.* Since the images of nature begin to overshadow those of destruction as the poem progresses, it can be inferred that this is done purposefully to show that life goes on after war, that it has value, and that it is delicate.

5. Part A: C: There are plenty of small details throughout the passage that indicate that Anne is full of energy and excited about being at Green Gables, if a little fearful that her stay might only be temporary. The reader does not get a sense of fear or anxiety, except when Anne thinks about not being able to stay. Her statements and dramatic views of everything around her do not show Anne to be shy, inactive, or wanting to be back at the orphanage.

Part B: There are several sentences that can be used as examples but one good choice is, "She had looked on so many unlovely places in her life, poor child; but this was as lovely as anything she had ever dreamed."

6. Part A: A: Each of the answer choices is a possible definition of the word "smart," but answer A is the only one that fits the context in which it is used. In the passage, Marilla is showing a little impatience for Anne's long, fanciful descriptions of Green Gables, and is giving Anne instructions for what she needs to do before she goes down to breakfast. The reader can infer that Marilla doesn't want Anne to waste any time. Therefore, A is the best choice.

Part B: A: All of the answer choices are synonyms of smart but based on the way it is used in the story "swift" makes the most sense.

7. C: Of all the answer choices, C makes the most sense, particularly in light of the following line: Marilla really did not know how to talk to the child, and her uncomfortable ignorance made her crisp and curt when she did not mean to be. The passage does not give the reader a sense that Marilla is suspicious or that she dislikes Anne, nor does it show her to be affectionate.

8. A: The fact that Anne's language in this section of the passage is very dramatic and reflects the romanticism of her earlier thoughts makes A the best choice here. There is no fear in the tone of this section, nor is there any indication that Anne is trying to prove herself.

9. C: Based on the sentence that follows the one in which "mortal" appears, it can be inferred that this word is describing the president's wound as fatal: *The wound is mortal. The President has been insensible ever since it was inflicted, and is now dying.*

10. A: This article has eight headlines, each containing more specific information than the one that comes before. Though some of the information presented in the headlines is clearly opinion, the overall message that is being communicated is informational: Lincoln was shot at Ford's theater; he's still alive, but not expected to survive. An attempt was also made on Secretary Seward's life.

11. B: The notation at the beginning of the article lets the reader know that the information provided is an official communication from the government. There is no author indicated at the beginning of the article. This is something that is included in most newspaper articles. However, the article is written in the first person, and the identity of the author is revealed at the end:

I have seen Mr. Seward, but he and Frederick were both unconscious.

Edwin M. Stanton, Secretary of War.

Two of the answer choices reference people mentioned in the article. Finally, *The New York Times* is the publisher, not the author.

12. A good summary of the article would be something close to this:

President Lincoln was shot by an assassin at Ford's Theater; the president is not expected to survive. Secretary Seward and his son were also attacked by an assassin at their home this evening. They remain unconscious, and their chances of survival are questionable. General Grant was scheduled to be at the theater, but changed his plans and was not harmed by the evening's events.

13. C: The first sentence expresses hope that the wounds inflicted upon Seward are not so severe that he would not be able to recover. The second sentence expresses the writer's fear that this hope may be misplaced, and it conveys that he is anxious about Seward's fate.

14. B: This sentence is the most grammatically correct, and does not change the meaning of the original sentence. Answer A repeats the grammatical errors. Answers C and D change the meaning of the original sentence.

15. A: This revision mirrors the concise and more formal tone of the rest of the essay. Answers B and D are too short, and do not provide the context and explanation of the author's ideas like the other sentences in the essay do. Answer C is too formal and passive, whereas the rest of the essay has some conversational aspects to the language, and is, for the most part, active.

16. C: This sentence directly supports the idea in the previous sentence about people taking their voting rights for granted. It shows that people don't have personal experience with being denied this right, and sets up the next sentence. Answers A and D do not make sense in the context of the discussion in this paragraph. Answer B does not support sentence 10 or lead into sentence 11 as effectively as answer C.

17. D: This sentence sums up Carter's position and reason for writing the essay. He is clearly arguing that people should take the right to vote more seriously than they do today, which is what this sentence says. The sentences that lead up to it provide context for this point.

18. B: Carter's essay talks a lot about people and attitudes during the Revolutionary War, but not much about how and why Americans today do not value their right to vote. Discussing this side of his argument will balance out his logic and make his essay more persuasive.

19. B: The three sentences preceding sentence 11 talk about what is on the U.S. side of the border. The sentences that follow talk about what is on the Mexican side. Sentence 11 transitions the discussion from one set of details to the other.

20. Part A: D: Answers A and B address ideas in the paragraph before Jordan's interpretation is mentioned, and don't apply here. Answer C provides a supporting detail, but answer D really shows why Jordan sees this image as sad.

Part B: C: This sentence explains why she feels sad. She explains Mexico gets as close to America as possible while America looks like they don't want to have anything to do with Mexico.

21. A: Comparing a complex relationship, such as the one between countries, to something less complex and seemingly unrelated, such as children playing, is an example of metaphor. Similes use "like" or "as" to compare two things. Alliteration uses similar starting sounds to create a specific effect.

22. B: All of the details that are given about people and events are presented from Lily's point of view. They are not objective, and reflect her reactions and opinions.

23. D: This detail comes from Lily's internal dialogue. The reader is privy to this since the story is told from her perspective. Everything is filtered through her perspective and knowledge. As a viewer of a film portrayal, this perspective is completely changed from that of a participant to that of an observer. The scene could plainly depict the details in answers A through C, but the detail in answer D is part of Lily's internal analysis, which would not be part of a film scene.

24. D: This part of the passage talks about how Jack Stepney keeps bringing Rosedale to fashionable places and events, and how he is snubbed for his actions. Rosedale is snubbed, too. Yet, he persists, saying "You'll see" to the naysayers. The answers that focus on Rosedale are incorrect, and there is no discussion of violence, as "sticking to one's guns" is used figuratively here.

25. C: The places where Rosedale's race is referenced and the line cited in this question allude to anti-Semitic attitudes toward the man.

26. B: Lincoln begins this speech by discussing the founding of our country and what the original purpose of the U.S. was. Then, he goes on to talk about how the U.S. is currently engaged in a war intended to fracture the nation, and he states that the battle being discussed was one large tragedy that came out of the war. Next, Lincoln says that his speech and even the memorial itself can't truly honor those who died, and that it's up to those who survived to continue the fight to ensure the nation does not break apart. Answer B best communicates this message.

27. C: The sentence in which this phrase is found is: The world will little note, nor long remember, what we say here, but can never forget what they did here. In this context, the phrase "the world will little note" means that no one outside of those in attendance or possibly those outside the country will pay attention to the speech or the ceremony. This eliminates all of the answer choices except C.

28. C: There is a comparison between the ideas of the Revolution and the Civil War in this speech. To facilitate understanding of this comparison, Lincoln has to set the stage by telling his audience about the past event he is referencing. This establishes the context of his message.

29. A: This line directly references the idea in the previous paragraph, which is that the U.S. is a nation that was created to ensure liberty and equality. This sentence talks about how the Civil War is testing whether or not a nation that was created to ensure liberty and equality can really survive.

English

Function of phrases

A phrase is a group of words in a sentence which can act as a single part of speech. There are noun phrases and verb phrases. The additional words make the meaning more specific, so there are also prepositional phrases, appositive phrases, and absolute phrases. Phrases are not complete sentences because they lack either a predicate or a subject. Phrases are parts of sentences, and sentences are frequently made up of one or more phrases. An example of a phrase is "the white horse" or "went very quickly." As you can see, neither phrase is a complete sentence. The first phrase lacks a predicate and the second phrase lacks a subject.

Clause

A clause is a word group that has a subject and a predicate and is used by itself or as part of a sentence. Unlike a phrase, a clause can be independent or stand by itself. It can also be dependent, which means it doesn't stand on its own and depends on an independent clause. Dependent clauses begin with a relative pronoun such as: that, who, whom, whose, which, where, when, or why; or a subordinating conjunction, such as: after, because, if, since, unless, to name a few. Dependent clauses can act as nouns, adjectives, and adverbs. *"If we knew what it was we were doing, it would not be called research, would it?"* (Albert Einstein). In this sentence, "If we knew what it was we were doing" is a dependent clause acting as a noun.

Simple vs. compound sentence

A simple sentence has one main clause with one subject and one predicate and no dependent clauses, while a compound sentence has two or more clauses, often joined by a comma and a conjunction, and sometimes by a semicolon. The addition of various phrases can sometimes make a simple sentence appear compound, but if the sentence has only one main clause, it is a simple sentence: For example: *Children around the world love soccer.* (Simple) *Children around the world love soccer, and it is the world's most popular sport.* (Compound)

Complex vs. compound-complex sentence

Adding dependent clauses to simple and compound sentences produces complex and compound-complex sentences. A complex sentence has one main clause and at least one dependent clause. A compound-complex sentence will have more than one main clause and at least one dependent clause.

"The path to my fixed purpose is laid on iron rails, on which my soul is grooved to run.'" (*Moby Dick*, Herman Melville) (Complex) *Although I love going to the movies, I haven't had very much time recently, and I don't know who to ask out.* (Compound-complex) It has two main clauses (I *haven't had much time, I don't know who to ask out)* and a dependent clause *(Although I love going to the movies).*

Identify what kind of sentence the following is and explain why this is true.

> George and his sister Veronica landed at the airport about 4:30 and left on the shuttle bus before we got there.

Many times looks can deceive. This is a simple sentence. There is one main clause. If it were a compound sentence, there would have to be two or more main clauses. It might be confusing because the simple subject and the simple predicate are expanded. It has a compound subject (*George and his sister Veronica*), compound verb *(landed and left),* adverbial phrase (*about 4:30*), and two prepositional phrases *(on the shuttle bus* and *before we got there*); therefore, despite the fact that it is a lengthy sentence, it is still just a simple sentence.

Describe how to rewrite the sentences below to include two dependent clauses.

> I graduated from high school. I was given a hunting knife. My grandfather once owned it.

The sentences are all short and are all about the same topic. They can be put together to make a more interesting sentence that will contain the same information by using clauses. Here is one way a writer could change the sentences to improve the expression of the sentence.

> After I graduated from high school, I was given a hunting knife that my grandfather once owned.

This revised sentence makes use of the dependent clause *After I graduated from high school* and the dependent clause *that my grandfather once owned* to make the passage more interesting to read.

Placing phrases and clauses within a sentence

Modifying phrases or clauses should be placed as closely as possible to the words they modify to ensure that the meaning of the sentence is clear. A misplaced modifier makes the meaning of a sentence murky. For instance, the meaning of *Walt barely missed the dog speeding down the street* becomes evident when the phrase is moved: *Speeding down the street, Walt barely missed the dog.* A dangling modifier doesn't have a word that it is modifying, so a word must be put into the sentence in order to complete its meaning. *Having arrived late for assembly, a written excuse was needed.* This sentence makes it sound as though the written excuse was late for assembly, so something needs to be added to the sentence. The meaning is clear when the name Jessica is added. *Having arrived late for assembly, Jessica needed a written excuse.* Here the phrase modifies Jessica.

Rewrite the following sentence so that it makes sense.

> A poem which received little acclaim when he was alive, today readers all over the world enjoy reading Walt Whitman's Leaves of Grass.

In this sentence it is not clear what the clause *A poem which received little acclaim when he was alive* is actually modifying because *poem* is too far away from the title of the poem, *Leaves of Grass.* The reader is forced to pause and think about what the sentence means, so the writing is unclear. Rewritten as *Readers all over the world today enjoy Walt Whitman's Leaves of Grass, a poem which received little acclaim when he was alive* places the modifier correctly so that the reader can immediately grasp the author's meaning. It is important when writing to check for dangling modifiers.

Using commas to separate coordinate adjectives

Coordinate adjectives are adjectives that apply equally to the noun they precede, and each one should be separated by a comma. Adjectives are coordinate if it sounds right to put the word *and* between them or if it sounds right when the order of the adjectives is reversed. *It was an old, decrepit house.* When there are more than two coordinate adjectives, a comma goes before the conjunction *and. The children were tired, hungry, and happy.* Adjectives that are not coordinate are not separated by a comma. *The cracked front window needs to be replaced.* The adjective *cracked* modifies *front window,* and the sentence does not sound right as *The cracked and front window,* so a comma is not needed.

Describe how to rewrite the following sentences, using commas to separate coordinate adjectives correctly.

> Yesterday, the brothers went to the new, Westbrook dog show. Their favorite dog was a young, black Labrador named Ralph. It was an enjoyable exciting dog show, and they will definitely come again.

Correctly written, the sentences should read: *Yesterday, the brothers went to the new Westbrook dog show. Their favorite dog was a young black Labrador named Ralph. It was an enjoyable, exciting dog show, and they will definitely come again.* The adjective *new* modifies *Westbrook dog show* so a comma is not needed. The same is true of *young, black Labrador,* where the adjective modifies *black Labrador,* a specific breed. Notice it would not make sense to say *young and black Labrador,* or *black, young Labrador. Enjoyable* and *exciting* are coordinate adjectives and are correctly separated by a comma.

Identify the incorrectly spelled words in the sentence that follows.

> The information you have is not relible since it comes from a sorce that has not been investegated.

The words that are misspelled are "relible," which would be "reliable," "sorce," which is spelled "source," and "investegated," which is spelled "investigated." It is important to learn to spell words correctly. One way to learn how to spell words is to learn how to sound out words. Break longer words down into syllables and into affixes and roots. Get the correct spelling from a dictionary and then practice that spelling. Take on only a few new words at a time; go on to new words only when you are certain you have mastered the current group. Practice using your new words in sentences. And learn the basic spelling rules, most famously "*I* before *e* except after *c*" (receive) as well as "drop the final *e*" (like, liking) and "double the last consonant" (stop, stopped). 7.3

Conventions of written language

The conventions of written language dictate using capitalization and punctuation correctly. Proper names, the first word of a sentence, and titles should be capitalized. Also, the names of countries, rivers, and states are all capitalized. Correct punctuation means using end marks, commas, semicolons, colons, and apostrophes correctly. The conventions of written language also say an author should make sure each sentence is complete. There should not be run-on or sentence fragments. Good penmanship is also important, so that the reader can understand what has been written; handwriting should be neat. Spelling is another important part of the conventions of written language. Words should be spelled correctly. To accomplish this, it may be necessary to use a dictionary. By using these conventions, an author will be able to communicate more clearly.

Discuss why the following sentence does not use the apostrophe correctly and explain why:

> The puppy stopped it's whimpering when we got home.

The sentence uses an apostrophe incorrectly. No apostrophe is needed after "it" because "it's" is in a possessive form. As it is written here "it's" means "it is"; it is a contraction but it has no place in this sentence. When considering whether an apostrophe is correctly placed, always ask yourself whether the apostrophe takes the place of the word "of," because that is what the apostrophe indicates: *the clothing store of the women* or *the orders of the customers.* No possessive is indicated in the sentence as it is written. It would be different if the sentence said: The puppy's whimpering stopped. Then the possessive form is required, since it is the whimpering *of* the puppy.

Edit the following sentence so that it expresses ideas precisely and concisely, and wordiness and redundancy are eliminated.

> If you go to the library on Sunday, you will find the library doors are locked and that the facility is closed on Sunday.

This sentence can be written just as effectively as: "The library is closed on Sundays." The expression "the library doors are locked" is redundant; it is not needed. What the writer is really saying is that the library is closed on Sunday. The writer also repeats the word Sunday when it is unnecessary and makes the sentence wordy. When writing, reread and revise your text after writing to make it is concise and not redundant. When writing a paragraph, or a longer passage, make sure that your main point is prominent within the first two to three sentences. Use supporting details to express more information about the main idea. And be sure to include an opening and ending to your essay. The ending should review what your main idea is about.

Using context clues

The term *context clue* refers to the words or phrases built into the sentences surrounding a new word. They allow you to guess the meaning of the word. Context clues may include examples of the new word, synonyms, antonyms, definitions, or contrasting information. By using context clues in the surrounding sentences, the reader can figure out approximately what the word means. A context clue indicating an example may contain the words *including* or *such as* or have a dash or a colon before stated information. A synonym is a word meaning almost the same thing as the new word. An antonym is a word with the opposite meaning to the new word. A definition will state exactly what the new word means. Contrasting information will include facts that are different from the new word.

Using context clues, determine the meaning of "gregarious" in the following excerpt.

> Beverly is the most gregarious person I have ever known. She loves people and spends a lot of her time talking to her friends and arranging get-togethers. She doesn't mind spending hours cooking as long as she knows that her house will be filled with people.

The word "gregarious" means sociable—someone who likes to talk with other people is gregarious or sociable. The context clues tell you this is the word's meaning. The excerpt says Beverly loves people and spends a lot of her time talking with friends and arranging get-togethers. It also says that she likes her house filled with people. And the excerpt says that Beverly is the opposite of her sister, who does not entertain.

Explain how the context words in the following sentences are clues to helping understand the meaning of the underlined word.

Emily was being very <u>blunt</u> with her brother. She didn't waste any time and came straight to the point.

There are numerous meanings to the word *blunt*. By reading carefully, you can figure out which meaning is appropriate here. The following sentence uses the phrases *waste any time* and *straight to the point*. These context clues support the fact that in this usage the word *blunt* most likely means short, curt, or even candid. It does not mean unsharpened or dull, which is another meaning of the word, because that would not make any sense; nor does it mean unfeeling, which is another common synonym, because that is not the sense that is being conveyed.

Knowledge of affixes and roots can be helpful in figuring out the meaning of a word

A root word is the original word, before it is added onto. An affix is a prefix, infix, or suffix that is added onto a root word. Often, the affixes in the English language come from Latin or Greek origins. A prefix is added before a root word, an infix is added to the middle of a root word, and a suffix is added to the end of a root word. When you look at the meaning of a root word and the meaning of any affixes added to the root word, you can figure out the approximate meaning of the word. For example, the root word "like" means to enjoy. The prefix "dis-"means not. The reader can therefore see that "dislike" means to not enjoy.

The word "inscription" is made up of three sections. The root "script" means "write" or "writing." It comes from the Latin word *scribere,* meaning *to write*. There are two affixes in the word. The prefix *in-* can mean various things such as "not," but also "on." In this case it means "on." The suffix *-tion* means "action" or "process." So put together the word "inscription" means "the act of writing on." Studying roots and affixes is important because it allows you to decode words you might not otherwise understand with relative ease.

Using specialized reference materials to determine the pronunciation of a word

A print or digital dictionary can be used as a means to find the correct pronunciation of words. The dictionary will have a guide that shows how to sound out the words, the symbols used to indicate the sounds, along with sample sounds (like the "i" in "pie," for instance). The dictionary can also be used to determine the meaning of the word, as well as its part of speech. The thesaurus is useful because it lists synonyms for all the various meanings a word can have, to help you clarify the precise meaning as used in the context of the text you are reading. Many books will have a glossary, placed at the end of the book, to help you with difficult or unfamiliar words used in the text.

Melissa used her dictionary to check the various meanings of the word "counsel." She found this entry:

> coun•sel ('kaun(t) suhl) *noun* 1. advice asked for and given. 2. a consultation. 3. guarded or private thoughts. 4. a lawyer who advises clients 5. a consultant *verb* 6. to advise 7. to consult with someone

Explain the definition of "counsel" in the following sentence.

> He decided to counsel with an expert about his financial problems.

The correct answer is meaning 7, "to consult with someone." Meanings 1 and 2 are incorrect because these are nouns, neither is a verb, which is used in the sentence. Meaning 6 is the opposite of the meaning in the sentence. When considering which meaning is being used, always check for context clues in the sentence or in the sentences before or after the sentence in which the word is used. Dictionaries also tell you how to pronounce words and often give the derivation of the word, although it is not given here.

Discuss the meaning of the word "baffle" in the following sentence.

> The criminal tried to baffle the detective by creating false clues and putting misleading fingerprints on the weapon.

The word "baffle" in this sentence means to confuse. The context of the sentence helps the reader figure this out because the sentence says that the criminal tried to baffle the detective. If you replace the word "baffle" with "confuse," it makes sense. There are other meanings of the word "baffle," but they do not fit in the sentence. To figure out the meaning of the word, use the context clues and then check the meaning of the word in a dictionary, either in print or online. A dictionary will also help you determine the meaning of the word by saying what part of speech it is when used in a particular instance. In this case the word "baffle" is used as a verb.

Explain what figure of speech is used in the following biblical passage and what it means:

> "For all flesh is as grass, and all the glory of man as the flower of grass." (1 Peter 1:24)

There are many instances of figurative language in the Bible. Here, a simile is used to compare human life to grass. Man is not really like grass, but, just as grass, and the flower of grass, grows and dies, so too will man grow and die. You can spot the use of a simile because the word "like" or "as" is often used. Similes differ from metaphors because metaphors do not use the word "like" or "as" to make the analogy. Other kinds of figures of speech or figurative language are hyperbole and personification. Hyperbole is an exaggeration that cannot be believed. Personification gives objects and animals human characteristics.

Using the relationships between words to better understand them

You can use the relationships between words to figure out the meaning by looking at how the words are used in the context of the passage. When you see a word that you do not know, try to figure it out from context clues. Then try to think of a synonym that would make sense in place of the word. Also think of an antonym to help you clarify its meaning. Word analogies can help enhance a word's meaning as well. A word analogy exists when there is a similarity or agreement between two words or they have a relationship to each other. Word analogies serve to sharpen your thinking skills. Word analogies are written as "word 1 is to word 2 as word 3 is to word 4" or "word 1: word 2 :: word 3 : _____," where you need to pick the best choice of a word to fit in the blank space, depending on what kind of analogy it is. When trying to figure out a word analogy, think about the kind of relationship that exists between the first two words and then try to duplicate the relationship in the second pair of words.

Describe what the relationships are among the following words: scalpel is to surgeon as transit is to surveyor (scalpel : surgeon :: transit : surveyor).

> In this word analogy, *scalpel* refers to an instrument or a tool that a surgeon commonly uses for a specific purpose (cutting). *Surgeon* is an occupation. Logically then, a *transit* is most likely an instrument or a tool used in an occupation. Therefore, *surveyor* has to denote an occupation. Even if you do not know what a transit is (an instrument used to measure horizontal and vertical angles), you can

deduce that the analogy is correct and that in this example the words are synonymous: instrument is to occupation as instrument is to occupation.

Distinguishing between the connotations of words with similar denotations

The connotation of a word is the unspoken meaning of the word beyond its dictionary meaning, or its denotation. It is the meaning that most people associate with that word; therefore it is a subjective interpretation of the meaning of the word, while a denotation is objective. For instance, the words "slender" and "skinny" both have a dictionary meaning of thin, but their connotations are quite different. "Slender" connotes thin as a stylish attribute, while "skinny" suggests an appearance that is undernourished, even unattractive. "Snake" is another example. The dictionary defines it as a reptile, but many people, when they hear the word "snake," associate it with someone who is not trustworthy.

Discuss the difference in the connotations between the words "wet" and "drenched."

"Wet" is a vague term; it could mean that you were caught in a rain drizzle or soaked to the bone. "Drenched," on the other hand, tells the reader that something is wet throughout. The connotations of "drenched" are much stronger than those of "wet." Drenched is an extreme condition, while wet is not. It is important to examine the context of the text where a word is to be used in order to choose an appropriate one. For instance, someone or something that is wet might be drenched, but it also might be moist or damp. Neither of these possibilities is remotely like drenched.

Improving comprehension

It is important to acquire and use accurately words and phrases at the appropriate level so as to improve comprehension. This helps the student to excel in the classroom as well as on standardized testing. A student who has to stop continually while reading in order to look up the meaning of words or who doesn't understand the part of speech being used is unable to focus on the overall meaning of the text and will therefore be unable to draw conclusions. Use of the dictionary and thesaurus and other digital tools helps the student to determine meanings, especially the meanings of prefixes, suffixes, and root words.

Practice Test

Practice Questions

Questions 1-8 pertain to the following passage:

An American Hero

(1) In the year 1912, the unsinkable Titanic sank, the United States territory of Arizona became a state, and my Great Uncle Charlie was born. (2) Charlie was born in a small town in Kentucky. (3) On a farm. (4) He grew up learning about the seasons, when to plant the seeds, and when the crops were ripe for picking. (5) His mornings were spent with his hands in dirt as he tended to the growing corps.

(6) When Charlie was only 12, his father died. (7) He had to quit school to take care of his family. (8) While other children were learning and playing at school, Charlie worked in factories to help pay for his mother and sisters to eat. (9) Irregardless of how he felt about having to work, Charlie never complained.

(10) On December 7, 1941, Japan attacked the American naval base at Pearl Harbor. (11) Charlie enlisted in the army when he was 30 years old, and went to fight in the war. (12) He fought in six major battles, including landing in Normandy on D-Day. (13) While he was in the army, Charlie joined the United States horseshoe team and became the champion of the european allies. (14) After the war, Charlie returned to Kentucky married a woman named Bethany, and had three children.

(15) Today, Charlie can still be found with his hands in the dirt. (16) He loves to work in the small garden beside his front porch. (17) The bright colors of ripening strawberries, tomatoes, and ears of corn can be seen next to the house with Charlie walking though the rows of crops with his watering can. (18) He tends to them with love. (19) Charlie watches over his family like the crops in the garden, and that is why he is my hero.

1. What is the BEST way to explain the information in sentences 2 and 3?

    a. Charlie was born in a small town in Kentucky. It was on a farm
    b. Charlie was born in Kentucky. In a small town and on a farm
    c. Charlie was born in a small town. In Kentucky, it was on a farm
    d. Charlie was born in a small Kentucky town on a farm

2. What change, if any, should be made to sentence 5?

    a. Change *corps* to *crops*
    b. Change *were* to *was*
    c. Insert a comma after *dirt*
    d. Make no change

3. What change, if any, should be made to sentence 9?

    a. Change *complained* to *complains*
    b. Change *irregardless* to *regardless*
    c. Delete the comma after *work*
    d. Make no change

- 153 -

4. What sentence could BEST follow and support sentence 10?

    a. Pearl Harbor is a naval base in Hawaii
    b. The USS Arizona was one of the battleships that sank
    c. This event directly led into the United States' involvement in World War II
    d.Charlie had never been to Hawaii

5. What change, if any, should be made to sentence 13?

    a. Change *european* to *European*
    b. Change *became* to *becomes*
    c. Insert a comma after *champion*
    d.Make no change

6. What change, if any, should be made to sentence 14?

    a. Change *returned* to *returns*
    b. Insert a comma after *Kentucky*
    c. Insert *and* after *Kentucky*
    d. Make no change

7. What change, if any, should be made in sentence 16?

    a. Change *loves* to *loved*
    b. Insert a comma after *garden*
    c. Change *beside* to *besides*
    d. Make no change

8. What change, if any, should be made in sentence 17?

    a. Change *colors* to *colours*
    b. Delete the comma after *strawberries*
    c. Change *though* to *through*
    d. Make no change

Questions 9 – 15pertain to the following story:

The Top Deck

(1) We walked outside through the sliding glass doors and waited in line for the large, double-decker red bus. (2) My family flew to London for a week in July to celebrate my sisters graduation. (3) She wore a blue cap and gown. (4) The sky was gray, and light puddles spotted the ground. (5) As the bus pulled up against the curb, dirty water splashed our feet.

(6) The driver's seat was on the opposite side of the bus, and the driver smiled at me when I showed him my ticket. (7) I looked out the window and realised that we were driving on the opposite side of the street. (8) All around us people who were on the wrong side of the street driving from what looked like the passenger seat. (9) The bus was filled with people. (10) Almost every seat was taken, and people were even standing in the aisle holding onto handrails and poles. (11) Their was a spiral staircase directly behind the driver, and we walked up it to try and find more seats. (12) There were two rows of seats upstairs and a large window that looked onto the streets. (13) For seats were open near the front of the bus and we hurried to get them.

(14) The bus stopped every few seconds, and each time I had to hold onto my seat to keep from sliding into the aisle. (15) "What street are we looking for?" my dad asked my mom. (16) "Oxford," she replied. (17) I looked out the giant window. (18) We passed a large building that was shaped like an egg, and we continued to travel. (19) The bus driver's voice came over the speakers. (20) "Now approaching Liverpool," he said

(21) My mom looked at my dad. (22) I grabbed my sister's arm, but she was busy taking pictures of the buildings out the window. (23) "Liverpool," my mom whispered with a worried look on her face. (24) "We're lost, aren't we?" my dad said.

9. What change, if any, should be made in sentence 2?

    a. Change *flew* to *flied*
    b. Change *week* to *weak*
    c. Change *sisters* to *sister's*
    d. Make no change

10. What change, if any, should be made in sentence 7?

    a. Change *realised* to *realize*
    b. Change *street* to *streat*
    c. Change *looked* to *look*
    d. Make no change

11. What change, if any, should be made in sentence 11?

    a. Delete the comma after *driver*
    b. Change *Their* to *There*
    c. Change *staircase* to *stair case*
    d. Make no change

12. What change should be made in sentence 13?

    a. Change *open* to *opened*
    b. Change *were* to *was*
    c. Change *For* to *Four*
    d. Change *hurried* to *hurried*

13. Which of the following is the BEST way to rewrite the ideas in sentence 8?

    a.All around us people were driving from what looked like the passenger seat, and they were driving on the opposite side of the street
    b. All around us people who were on the wrong side of the street, driving from what looked like the passenger seat
    c. All around us people were driving on the wrong side of the street. Driving from what looked like the passenger seat
    d. All around us people were driving from what looked like passenger seat, they were on the opposite side of the street

14. Which sentence does not belong in this essay?

    a. Sentence 20
    b. Sentence 6
    c. Sentence 13
    d. Sentence 3

15. What is the BEST transition word or phrase that could be added to the beginning of sentence 19?

  a. However
  b. Once in a while
  c. Additionally
  d. After a while

Questions 16 -21 pertain to the following story:

Longhorn Café

(1) Last Saturday night my dad took me to watch the Longhorns play football in Austin. (2) It was a cool evening, and the orange-painted stadium was filled with screaming fans. (3) Even though we live in San Antonio, my dad has always been a dedicated Longhorns fan, and he wears his orange proudly.

(4) We arrived in Austin early. (5) "Traffic," my dad said as his only explanation. (6) He parked the truck down a small side street and motions for me to get out and follow him. (7) "I want to take you someplace," he said. (8) "I used to come here all the time when I was in college." (9) We walked up to a small building with a large patio off to the side. (10) A large tree with low branches spread across the patio and connected with the roof. (11) The leaves were beginning to change colors, and it was like sitting under a leafy canopy.

(12) We sat at a table outside on a rusting rocking bench beside an abandoned bathtub. (13) Stands of colored lights hung across the patio. (14) Wrapped around the tree. (15) "What is this place?" I asked. (16) My dad smiled and pointed to a sign bordered with colored lights. (17) "Spider Café," he said. (18) All around us, people were drinking coffee and staring at them computer screens. (19) Our waiter was named Chris, and he had a long beard, wore a dirtied apron, and carried empty coffee mugs.

(20) The waited came up to us, and my dad ordered himself a latte and a sweet drink for me. (21) My dad looked around the patio and smiled. (22) He leaned into the bench and placed his hand on the side of the bathtub. (23) He didn't even mind when he spilled coffee onto his favorite orange shirt. (24) "You'll love it here," he said, "when you are a Longhorn football player."

16. What change, if any, should be made in sentence 5?

  a. Delete the comma after *traffic*
  b. Insert a comma after *said*
  c. Change *said* to *says*
  d. Make no change

17. What change should be made in sentence 6?

  a. Change *parked* to *park*
  b. Change *street* to *Street*
  c. Insert a comma after *street*
  d. Change *motions* to *motioned*

- 156 -

18. What revision, if any, is needed in sentences 13 and 14?

    a. Strands of colored lights hung across the patio wrapped, around the tree
    b. Strands of colored lights hung across the patio and wrapped around the tree
    c. Strands of colored lights hung. Across the patio, wrapped around the tree
    d. No revision is needed

19. What change, if any, should be made in sentence 18?

    a. Change *them* to *their*
    b. Delete the comma after *us*
    c. Insert a comma after *and*
    d. Make no change

20. Where is the best placement for sentence 19?

    a. After sentence 22
    b. After sentence 20
    c. Before sentence 18

    d.No change is needed

21. What change, if any, should be made in sentence 20?

    a. Change *ordered* to *orders*
    b. Change *himself* to *hisself*
    c. Change *waited* to *waiter*
    d. Make no change

Questions 22– 28 pertain to the following story:

Strike Three

(1) As I stared down at the hitter in the batters box, I remembered what my dad had said to me. (2) "Shut everything out." (3) I focused on the glove in front of me. (4) I looked into the deep, blackened pocket, and sawed my target. (5) The batter tapped his bat against the sides of his cleats, and rested the bat on his shoulders. (6) With hard eyes, he stared back at me.

(7) I kicked the front of my cleat into the bright white rubber on the pitching mound and took a deep breath. (8) Shut everything out," he had said. (9) Slowly the noises disappeared. (10) I could no longer hear the shouts from the parents in the stands. (11) In my head, I silenced the cheers from both dugouts. (12) The umpire did not exist. (13) There were no players, no coaches, not even a catcher. (14) There was just me. (15) The ball and the glove.

(16) I took a deep breath and brought my hands together at my chest. (17) I looked over at first base, but there was no runner. (18) In one motion, my feet left the rubber and connected with ground. (19) Dirt flew in the air as my arm rotated forward and released the ball in front of me. (20) I watched as the ball spun and landed into glove with a hard crack. (21) The umpire shot up from his crouched position and pointed his finger to the right and yelled, "Strike Three!"

(22) The noises came back. (23) The crowd cheered in the stands and I could here stomping feet. (24) My teammate clapped his hand to its glove and ran toward me.

(25) My coach raised a first into the air in celebration. (26) I was surrounded by my teammates, and they were patting me on the back. (27) My dad was sitting on a bleacher behind home plate. (28) He raised his thumb to me and smiled as I ran off the field with my teammates.

22. What change, if any, should be made in sentence 1?
    a. Change *stared* to *starred*
    b. Change *dad* to *Dad*
    c. Change *batters* to *batter's*
    d. Make no change

23. What change should be made in sentence 4?
    a. Change *blackened* to *blacked*
    b. Change *sawed* to *saw*
    c. Delete the comma after *deep*
    d. Change *into* to *in to*

24. What change should be made in sentence 8?
    a. Change *everything* to *every thing*
    b. Delete the comma after *out*
    c. Change the comma after *out* to a period
    d. Insert quotation marks before *Shut*

25. What is the best way to combine sentence 14 and sentence 15?
    a. There was just the ball, the glove, and me
    b. There was just me, the ball, and the glove
    c. There was just me and the ball and the glove
    d. Make no change

26. What change, if any, should be made in sentence 23?
    a. Change *cheered* to *cheer*
    b. Change *here* to *hear*
    c. Change *could* to *can*
    d. Make no change

27. What sentence could BEST follow and support sentence 22?
    a. My foot was still planted hard into the ground
    b. The sounds came flooding into my ears as I looked up
    c. I felt good
    d. The umpire took off his mask and started walking toward the fence

28. What is the BEST transition word that could be added to the beginning of sentence 26?
    a. However
    b. Consequentially
    c. Soon
    d. Therefore

Questions 29– 35 pertain to the following passage:

Imagine a Better World

(1) My favorite song is "imagine" by John Lennon. (2) It was released in 1971. (3) It is one of the few famous songs that John Lennon recorded and sang alone. (4) For the majority of his career, John Lennon was a member of an iconic rock band called the Beatles, a band that changed the music industry. (5) The Beatles had a lot of success in their career, with popular songs such as "I Want to Hold Your Hand," "Come Together," "Let it Be," and "Here Comes the Sun." (6) After the band decided to separate, John Lennon became a solo artist as well as an promoter for peace.

(7) "Imagine" tells the story of Lennons dream of peace in the world. He asks the listener to imagine different situations. (8) He says to imagine that there are no countries, religions, or possessions. (9) He says, "I wonder if you can." (10) This line strikes me the most I try to imagine such a world. (11) When talking about no possessions, he continues and says, "No need for greed or hunger." (12) It is a great line. (13) Throughout the song, he says, "Imagine all the people." (14) And he gives examples. (15) At first he says, "living for today," and then moves on to say, "living life in peace," and finally, "sharing all the world."

(16) My favorite part of the song is the chorus. (17) Lennon says, "You may say I'm a dreamer, but I'm not the only one. (18) I hope someday you'll join us, and the world will be as one." (19) When I really listen to the words of this song, I realize that "Imagine" is so much more than something that sounds nicely. (20) Lennon is saying something very important and suggesting ways in which the world can live in peace. (21) Because of this song, I am a dreamer as well, and I join John Lennon in the fight for world peace.

29. What change, if any, should be made in sentence 1?

    a. Change *favorite* to *favourite*
    b. Change *imagine* to *Imagine*
    c. Insert a comma after *song*
    d. Make no change

30. What change should be made in sentence 6?

    a. Change *separate* to *separated*
    b. Insert a comma after *artist*
    c. Change *solo* to *Solo*
    d. Change *an* to *a*

31. What change, if any, should be made in sentence 7?

    a. Change *Lennons* to *Lennon's*
    b. Change *dream* to *dreamt*
    c. Insert a comma after *peace*
    d. Make no change

32. What is the BEST way to revise sentence 10?

    a. This line strikes me the most as I try to imagine such a world.

- 159 -

b.This line strikes me the most, I try to imagine such a world.
c. This line strikes me, the most. I try to imagine such a world.
d. No revision needed.

33. What is the BEST way to combine sentence 13 and sentence 14?

a. Throughout the song, he says "Imagine all the people" and he gives examples.
b. Throughout the song, he says, "Imagine all the people," and he gives examples.
c. Throughout the song he says Imagine all the people, and he gives examples.
d. Throughout the song he says Imagine all the people and he gives examples.

34. What change, if any, should be made in sentence 18?

a. Insert a quotation mark before *I*
b. Move the period after the quotation marks
c. Change *you'll* to *youl'l*
d. Make no change

35. What change should be made in sentence 19?

a. Delete the comma after *song*
b. Change *something* to *some thing*
c. Change *nicely* to *nice*
d. Change *realize* to *realized*

Answers and Explanations

1. D: because this sentence is the simplest way to explain where Charlie was born. A is not correct because two sentences are not necessary. The additional subject and verb are unnecessary to express the idea. B is not correct, because *In a small town and on a farm* is a fragment. C is not correct, because the sentences contain awkward wording. The sentences need to be combined in order to express the idea in the simplest form.

2. A: because in this sentence, *crops* has been misspelled as *corps*. B is not correct, because the subject of the sentence, *mornings*, is plural. Therefore, the verb also must be plural for correct subject verb agreement. C is not correct, because this sentence does not need a comma.

3. B: because irregardless is not a word. The correct word is *regardless.* A is not correct because *complains* is in the present tense, while the rest of the paragraph is in the past tense. C is not correct, because a comma is needed after an introductory clause.

4. C: because this sentence supports both sentence 10 and sentence 11. The sentence supports the cause and effect idea that the attack on Pearl Harbor prompted the United States to become involved in the war, which caused Charlie to enlist in the army. A is not correct. Although this sentence provides new information, it does not link and support sentences 10 and 11. B is not correct. Although this sentence provides new information, it does not link and support sentences 10 and 11. D is not correct. Although this sentence provides new information, it does not link and support sentences 10 and 11.

5. A: because *European* is a proper noun and must be capitalized. B is not correct, because *becomes* is in the present tense, and the rest of the paragraph is written in the past tense. C is not correct, because a comma is not needed after *champion.*

6. B: because this sentence uses commas in a series as it lists aspects of Charlie's life after the war. Both *returned to Kentucky* and *married a woman named Bethany* are events that have happened and therefore need to be separated by a comma. A is not correct. *Returns* is in the present tense, and the rest of the paragraph is written in the past tense. C is not correct. The correct sentence uses commas in a series, and therefore only uses one *and* in the sentence.

7. D: because the sentence is correct as written. A is not correct. Although the rest of the essay is written in the past tense, the last paragraph begins with *Today* and is written in the present tense. Therefore, *loves* is correct. B is not correct, because this sentence does not need a comma. C is not correct. Both *beside* and *besides* are prepositions, but *beside* means "next to" and *besides* means "in addition to" or "other than." *Beside* is used in this sentence as "next to."

8. C: because in this sentence, *through* has been misspelled as *though*. A is not correct, because *colors* is spelled correctly. B is not correct, because this sentence needs a comma after *strawberries,* since the sentence contains a list and uses commas in a series.

9. C: In this sentence, *Sister's* is possessive and requires an apostrophe. A is not correct. *Flew* is the correct past tense of *fly*. B is not correct, because *week* is a noun and is spelled correctly.

10. A: because *realized* is misspelled in this sentence. B is not correct, because *street* is spelled correctly. C is not correct, because *look* is in the present tense, while the essay is written in past tense.

11. B: because a homonym has been misused. *There* is used to indicate a physical or abstract place, while *their* is used to indicate possession. A is not correct, because this sentence has two independent clauses joined by the conjunction *and*, and a comma is used before the conjunction. C is not correct, because *staircase* is one word.

12. C: because a homonym has been misused. *Four* is a number. A is not correct, because in this sentence *open* is used as a noun rather than a verb and does not need to be in the past tense. B is not correct. *Were* is plural, and *was* is singular. The subject of the sentence, *seats*, is plural; therefore, the verb also must be plural for correct subject verb agreement. D is not correct, because *hurried* is spelled correctly.

13. A: because this rewording of this sentence makes the meaning clear and is grammatically correct. B is not correct because this sentence is a fragment. C is not correct because the second sentence is a fragment. D is not correct because this sentence is a run-on sentence.

14. D: because this sentence this sentence provides new information that is not important to the rest of the essay. Answers A, B, and C are incorrect, because all of these sentences present content that is important to the essay.

15. D: In the previous sentence, the phrase *we continued to travel*, suggests a passage of time. A proper transition into the next sentence would involve the acknowledgement that time has passed. A is not correct because *however* is not a good transition into the sentence. B is not correct. Although *once in a while* relates to time, it does not transition well into the sentence given the context of the previous sentence. C is not correct. *Additionally* is not a good transition into the sentence because it does not indicate a passage of time.

16. D: because the sentence is correct as written. A is not correct, because a comma is needed before the closing quotation when the sentence is not completed with the quotation. B is not correct because this sentence does not need a comma. C is not correct because *says* is in the present tense, and the essay is written in the past tense.

17. D: because *motions* is in the present tense, and the rest of the essay is written in the past tense. B is not correct because *street* is not used in this sentence as a proper noun and does not need to be capitalized. C is not correct. A comma is unnecessary because the second sentence is not an independent clause.

18. B: because this sentence is grammatically correct as written. A is not correct. The comma is misplaced and disrupts the sentence. C is not correct because the second sentence is a fragment. D is not correct because sentence 14 is a fragment.

19. A: because *their* indicates possession; *them* does not. *Computer screens* belong to the subject, *people*. B is not correct. *All around us* is an introductory clause and needs a comma. C is not correct. *Staring at them computer screens* is not an independent clause and therefore does not need a comma.

20. B: because the sentence provides additional information about the waiter. The sentence should be placed after the waiter has been introduced in sentence 20. A is not correct. The subject of the paragraph has shifted to the father at sentence 21, and therefore a sentence involving information about the waiter would be out of place after sentence 22. C is not correct. Sentence 18 provides setting information. A sentence involving information about the waiter before this sentence would be out of place. D is not correct. This sentence provides additional information about the waiter and should not conclude a paragraph.

21. C: because *waiter* has been misspelled. A is not correct. *Orders* is in the present tense, and the essay is written in the past tense. B is not correct because *himself* is the correct word, while *hisself* is not a word.

22. C: In this sentence, *batter's* is possessive and needs an apostrophe. A is not correct because *stared*, the past tense of the verb, *stare*, is spelled correctly. B is not correct. In this sentence, *dad* is not a proper noun, since it is not used as a name. *My* before *dad* indicates that it is not a proper noun.

23. B: because *saw* is the correct past tense of the verb, *see*. A is not correct because *blackened* is the correct adjective. C is not correct. A comma is needed to separate adjectives when each adjective separately describes the noun. D is not correct. *Into* is spelled correctly.

24. D: It is correct because the quotation marks after *out* indicate dialogue. Quotation marks are needed before *Shut* to begin the dialogue. A is not correct. When used as a noun, *everything* is one word. B is not correct. A comma is needed before the closing quotation when the sentence is not completed with the quotation. C is not correct. The sentence is not completed with the quotation, and therefore it needs a comma rather than a period before the closing quotation.

25. A: because this sentence is grammatically correct. B is not correct. When using the pronoun, *me*, in a series, it is always placed at the end of the series. C is not correct. The repetition of *and* is not grammatically correct. The nouns need to be separated using commas in a series.

26. B: It is correct because a homonym has been misused. *Hear* indicates the act of hearing and listening. *Here* indicates location. A is not correct. *Cheer* is in the present tense, and the rest of the essay is in the past tense. C is not correct. *Can* is in the present tense, and the rest of the essay is in the past tense.

27. B: It is correct because this sentence supports both sentence 22 and 23. The preceding sentence discusses noises coming back. The next logical sentence should have something to do with noises. A is not correct. Although this sentence provides new information, it does not link and support sentences 22 and 23. C is not correct. Although this sentence provides new information, it does not link and support sentences 22 and 23. D is not correct. Although this sentence provides new information, it does not link and support sentences 22 and 23.

28. C: because a proper transition into the next sentence would involve the acknowledgement that time has passed. A is not correct. *However* is not a good transition into this sentence since it does not require a shift in ideas. B is not correct. *Consequentially* is not a good transition into this sentence since it presents no cause and effect. D is not correct. *Therefore* is not a good transition into this sentence since it presents no cause and effect.

29. B: because *imagine* is a proper noun. As the title of a song, it requires capitalization. A is not correct. *Favorite* is spelled correctly. C is not correct. *My favorite song* is not an introductory clause, so a comma is not needed.

30. D: It is correct because in the sentence, the article *an* is followed by a noun, *promoter*. *Promoter* begins with a consonant and a consonant sound and therefore must be followed by the article *a*. A is not correct. The verb in this sentence is *decided*, not *separate*, and therefore *separate* does not need to be in the past tense like the rest of the paragraph. B is not correct because the comma is unnecessary. C is not correct. *Solo* is not a proper noun and does not need to be capitalized.

31. A: because *Lennon* is possessive in this sentence; therefore, it requires an apostrophe. B is not correct. In this sentence, *dream* is a noun rather than a verb, so it does not need to be in the past tense. C is not correct, because a comma is unnecessary.

32. A: because the sentence is missing the article *as*. This is the simplest way to express the idea of the sentence. B is incorrect because this sentence is not grammatically correct. C is incorrect because the first sentence is grammatically incorrect.

33. B: because this is the simplest way to express the idea in a grammatically correct sentence. F is incorrect because a comma is missing after *song* and after *people*. H is incorrect because a comma is missing after *song*, and quotation marks are missing around the quotation, *"Imagine all the people."* J is not correct. A comma is missing after *song* and after *people*, and quotation marks are missing around the quotation, *"Imagine all the people."*

34. D: It is correct because the sentence is correct. A is not correct. This sentence is part of a longer quotation that began in the previous sentence. Since the quotation is continuing, the sentence does not begin with quotation marks. B is not correct. In a quotation, the punctuation is placed before the ending quotation marks. C is not correct. *You'll* is the correct contraction of *you will*.

35. C: because in this sentence *nice* is an adjective rather than an adverb. It describes the noun, *sounds*, not the verb. A is not correct. *When I really listen to the words of this song* is an introductory clause, and a comma is needed after the clause. B is not correct. *Something* is one word when used as a noun. D is not correct. Although most of the essay is in the past tense, the final paragraph is in the present tense. *Realized* is in the past tense.

Writing

Producing clear and coherent writing

The first step to producing clear and coherent writing is to plan first what you are going to say, how you want to say it, and who your audience is. Think about the tone you want to project. While writing, develop and organize arguments in a logical order. Thoughts should be organized into paragraphs. Sentences should be precise. Support ideas with evidence, and mention opposing points of view as well. Then follow up with a conclusion. Be careful of too much repetition and use punctuation correctly to emphasize points. After writing, check for errors, both mechanical and in content, and make necessary revisions. Many find it useful to read the text aloud as a final guidepost.

Constructive criticism

A process of ongoing, constructive criticism of previous work from peers and adults in the classroom can help you improve your writing. It is often easier for others to see what needs to be improved than for the writer himself. Having a brief plan in mind before starting to write is useful, so that you know what points you want to cover. After completing your writing, leave it alone for a while. When you look at it again, your mind will be much fresher. Revising your writing means rethinking it; ask yourself if the reader will understand what you are trying to say. Did you achieve your purpose? Editing involves looking for better use of vocabulary, grammar, and sentence structure. Then the process of rewriting begins. At that time, it is possible that you may decide to try another approach. You may need to revise your main idea and make the supporting details clearer. Make sure that your work will create interest in the audience that you will choose. Ask for help from appropriate adults to review and critique or correct your text.

Conducting a short research project

When conducting a short research project to answer a question, start by making a list of key words that relate to the question at hand. These words will be used by a search engine to begin the search for information. The words can also be used when utilizing an encyclopedia, either in print or online, or searching through back issues of journals, magazines, or newspapers. Whatever the source of the information, make sure it is timely and not dated. The sources that are used should be cited properly, following the standards of the Modern Language Association (MLA).Questions that are posed in the research project should be clear and explicit. Use the information that you have researched to expand your investigation by creating other focus questions.

Using the Internet

There are many electronic sources now available for students to get written works of all kinds published online at no cost. Technology also allows for easy access to sources used in a writing project. These sources can be cited by listing the URL, title, author, and date retrieved. The growth of chat rooms and topic websites now allows for an unprecedented exchange of information. In addition, many free tools are accessible that provide software to allow people to work together on all kinds of projects, no matter how far apart they are geographically. Students can find discussion groups, file sharing networks, social networking sites, blogs, and task management sites, all of which foster interaction and collaboration.

Gathering relevant information from multiple print and digital sources

Gathering relevant information from multiple print and digital sources requires judging, first of all, how much information is necessary for the size of the project. The researcher should then think about how knowledgeable her audience is on the subject. While researching, it is important to maintain a balance between being too specific, with unnecessary details, and being too general, with oversimplifications. It is also important to check the age of the source material. There are many sources a researcher can turn to the Internet, journals, newspapers, text books, even works by other students, to name a few. Using search engines makes the task easier; generally one query will bring up all the data needed. Plagiarism, or using another's words without any acknowledgment, can be avoided by giving credit to works cited using MLA (Modern Language Association) standards.

Historical fiction

Historical fiction can often stray from historical reality in order to tell a story and make the historical event more interesting to the reader. While being true for the most part, historical fiction may take poetic license when it comes to individual characters or the details of a situation. For instance, a story might take place in 19th-century Britain. While the author would have the details correct as to when and where an event took place, the author might fictionalize a character that did not actually live during this period. Or the author could take a person who was mentioned in research and turn this person into a character of his or her liking. When reading historical fiction, you need to always remind yourself that all the details mentioned might not be accurate; this is why it is called historical fiction rather than history.

Reading literary nonfiction

Reading literary nonfiction works requires digging for the author's point of view. You need to use critical thinking skills to determine whether the reasoning is sound. Ask yourself whether you can discern what the central idea of the passage is. Does the language seem confident and persuasive? Can you distinguish between what is fact and what is opinion? Look for statistics and representative examples to back up arguments and support the author's claims. Look for evidence of bias, omissions, and stereotypes; their presence severely limits the relevance of the work. Check sources to make sure that the information is timely.

Make writing a habit

Writing is important in all aspects of adult life. Therefore, it is important to learn to write routinely so that writing comes easily and smoothly. Teaching yourself that writing can be a habit means that you will understand that the more often you write, the better your writing will become. Once you understand the process of writing (making notes, drafting, writing, editing, revising), you will understand the concept of writing for different kinds of audiences and writing longer, more thoroughly researched articles as well as shorter, quick articles, and you will understand that some topics require much more effort and time than others. Learning the skills necessary to master the art of writing for specific disciplines leads to greater recognition in any field you choose.

Analyze the claim made in the statement below:

> The Good Value Supermarket should be closed. It has been cited numerous times for failure to live up to cleanliness standards. I have been to the market and seen firsthand examples of unclean practices. We should act at once.

The claim may or may not be valid. While the statement says that the market has been cited numerous times for failure to live up to cleanliness standards, it does not give a source for this claim, which lessens its import. The statement then includes a firsthand account, which may or may not be accurate and then resorts to an emotional plea, neither of which strengthen the claim. When making a claim, the argument should be well researched, and sources should be used to back up the claim and make it a valid one. This is not the case in the statement that was given.

Tell which of the following words fits best in the blank and why: "because" or "otherwise:"

The lawyer tried to prove his client was innocent; ___he would go to prison.

"Otherwise" is the correct choice because it creates a relationship of contrast. The word "because" suggests a cause and effect relationship, which does not exist in the sentence. The same is true of the word "since." It is important to understand the relationship between what might happen and what is happening in order to ensure that your sentences have a logical flow. Here the relationship that exists is between opposing possibilities. Cause and effect relationships indicate what will happen as a result of something taking place, which is not the case here. With the addition of the word "otherwise," there is a natural, logical flow in the sentence.

Harold was writing a presentation on the reasons that schools should require uniforms. He needed a closing statement. Describe how he should go about writing a conclusion.

He should review all of the arguments that he has made for requiring uniforms and then he should make a general final statement about why he feels it would be a good idea. He can use a personal appeal here and hope that the reader will agree with his point of view. It is probably best not to include opposing points of view in the conclusion. The conclusion that Harold writes should sound like the ending of the presentation. It should not introduce new material or leave items open for further discussion.

Here is the beginning of a report that Brad is writing. Discuss how to improve it.

Bats are interesting animals. They have wings. They eat insects. I saw a bat once when I was camping in the woods. We went into a cave and there were a lot of them sleeping.

This beginning is not very strong. It starts out with a statement, then has two facts about bats, but then goes into a personal accounting of when the writer saw a bat. The opening of a report should have a broad statement about the topic and then discuss what areas of the topic will be covered in the report. Personal accounts usually have little place in a formal report that is supposed to be based on a person's research, although a personal account might be a way of making the topic more interesting to the reader. But it does not take the place of solid research.

Decide which event happens first.

Margo was falling into a pool of water. Or was she flying in the sky? Maybe she was a dragon. She couldn't be sure. She thought about what had happened earlier. She ate the strange candy and she felt giddy. What was happening to her? She had no idea.

It is important to figure out the sequence of events in order to grasp what is happening in the passage. It says that Margo was falling into a pool of water and then it says that she was flying in the sky. Then it says she may have been a dragon. But the key to the sequence is in the word "earlier": "She thought about what had happened earlier." This tells us that the next event was the first in a progression of events. She ate the candy first. Then she felt giddy. So the reader can figure out the sequence of events and then better grasp the meaning of the story.

Persuasive Text

Introducing arguments

When introducing arguments for or against a claim in a persuasive text, be sure that the argument is thoroughly researched and thought through. Make sure to organize your argument; the best way to do this is to make notes or an outline. Put the claim first and then list the reasons and evidence that you have to support the claim. Make sure the reasons and evidence follow from each other so that they are in a logical order. Delete any reasons or claims that cannot be substantiated by outside sources. By doing this you will be prepared to make a presentation that is compelling and convincing.

Making a claim

When making a claim, you will need to research arguments in support of it that come from trustworthy sources. It is not enough to research a claim on the Internet because many sources are doubtful. You will need to find information that can be verified by several objective sites if you are doing research on the Internet. Another avenue is to find authorities in a field who have written or spoken on the topic that you are presenting so that you can quote these people. These authorities should have substantial degrees in their field as well as a vast experience so that their opinions will have credence and respect. Be sure to cite any information that you use to support a claim correctly. And make sure to present your arguments in a logical manner so that they will be easily understood by the listener or reader.

Creating cohesion

When writing, it is important to phrase your sentences so that they follow logically and so that the claim and the evidence are clearly identified and related. Words or phrases such as "because," "since, "as a result of," and "as a consequence" or "consequently" all suggest a causality that may exist between a reason and a claim. Clauses can also be utilized to show relationships. "Because the temperature of the water is lower, the fish become dormant" shows causality between the reason and the effect. When writing, make sure to recheck your sentences to ensure that there is a natural flow and that relationships between causes and effects are evident and logical.

Formal style

When writing a persuasive essay or other kind of formal paper, a formal style needs to be maintained throughout. The requirements of a formal writing style include the use of the third person, rather than first or second person. This lends a more serious tone to a paper and keeps personal feelings from affecting the integrity of the text. A formal style also requires proper English conventions as well as language that is professional and without prejudice. A formal style does not allow for colloquialism or a casual conversational tone. It requires that the author remain at all times objective, giving a presentation that is based on logic and reason.

Read the following passage. Suggest how to make it more formal.

> I've read in magazines that there is a lot of talk these days about artificial sweeteners. It's hard to tell if they are good for you or not. I need to lose weight. Plus I'm worried I'll get diabetes. So I think I am going to try some.

The style of the passage is very informal and personalized; the first person is used exclusively. Sentences are all short and simple, and there is little substance.

Here is one way to rewrite it.

> There have been reports published recently concerning the use of non-carbohydrate synthetic sugars, and the controversy that surrounds whether or not these products constitute a health risk. Individual use has been shown to be prompted primarily by a desire for weight loss, as well as to deter the onset of type 2 diabetes.

To make the passage more meaningful and more authoritative, third-person narration is substituted. Complex sentences are utilized. A higher, more specific vocabulary level is introduced—instead of *artificial sweeteners,* the substance is labeled scientifically: *non-carbohydrate synthetic sugars.* The result is that the passage is more authoritative. The information is presented in a more formal, structured manner.

Importance of having a conclusion

It is imperative to have a conclusion to any written or spoken presentation that sums up the overall intention of the text and gives the audience a sense of closure. The conclusion of a persuasive text should review the most important points that have been made in the presentation and the reasoning and arguments that the author has made to support them. The conclusion should not make the reader feel that there is more information to follow, but rather set the tone for the ending of the argument by being reassuring and providing an ending to the theme of the text. A good conclusion is important to the effectiveness of a text.

Informational or Explanatory Text

Introducing a topic

When writing an informational or explanatory text, the author will need to introduce the topic that the text will be about. This can be done in a number of ways. Often the topic is introduced as a topic sentence with supporting details coming after it. Very frequently authors attempt to find a way to make the topic relevant to what is going on in the modern world, even if the topic refers to something that is in the past, so that it will be immediately interesting to the reader. Along with introducing the topic, the author should preview the ideas and concepts that will be discussed by showing how relevant they are to the main topic. Many authors preview these concepts by showing how they affect everyday life. This also makes the text more relevant to the reader.

Developing a topic

When an author develops a topic in an informational or explanatory text, the author must use relevant facts that will act as supporting details to the main topic. The topic may be included in a topic sentence and then followed by supporting details. These supporting details should be concrete facts that have been researched and are accurate. In addition to facts, it is a good idea to use quotes from experts in a field that is relevant to the topic. This will lend even greater meaning as well as interest for the audience. Examples, charts, and multimedia techniques will also enhance the presentation, but take care that the multimedia techniques support the main idea and are not a substitute for supporting details.

Analyze the beginning of this informational text and tell how to improve it:

> Some people think that boys and girls should go to different schools. They give several reasons for this opinion. Girls participate more when boys aren't around. Boys and girls concentrate better when the opposite sex is not around.

This seems like a good start to an informational text. The first sentence sets out the topic. It tells what the report is going to be about. It also includes two supporting details to tell more about the topic. This is one way to introduce and develop a topic in a report or other informational or explanatory text. What should come are more supporting details and also sources for the information that is cited; this would make the report stronger and give it credence.

Organize ideas

There are numerous ways to organize the ideas that are presented in an informational or explanatory text. Certainly it is important to provide any definitions of concepts that might be unknown to the audience, but then the author needs to decide how to organize the material. Some authors choose to classify material; others prefer to use a compare and contrast or cause and effect organization. Whatever the organization that is chosen, the author may also opt to use headings and graphics, such as charts and/or tables. Multimedia alternatives, including audios and videos, can supply a range of ways to present new material that will be appealing to the audience as well as being effective.

Read the following passage. Explain which organization pattern would seem to be the best choice and why:

> Anita is writing an essay on crocodiles and alligators. She has compiled a long list of what they look like, what they eat, where they live, and who their predators are. She is unsure of how to organize her report.

A compare and contrast order would seem to be the best idea, since she would very easily be able to compare the ways the crocodiles and alligators look, what they eat, where they live, and who their predators are . The compare and contrast order works best when an author is writing about two animals, things, or people, since it allows the information about each one to be compiled in an orderly way that would be easy for the reader to understand. In addition to the order, Anita could use headings and charts to further organize the material. Audios and videos might also be a good supplement to the essay.

Using appropriate transitions

When writing an informational or explanatory text, it is important to use appropriate transitions that will give cohesion to the text and also help clarify the relationships among ideas and concepts. For example, make sure to use transition words or phrases, such as "therefore," "consequently," and "as a result of," to show causality between ideas. Words such as "however," "on the other hand," "but," "in contrast," and "similarly" show a comparison and contrast relationship. Transition words and expressions that show examples include "for example," "for instance," "namely," and "that is." The order of importance can also be shown through transitions, such as "at first," "former," "latter," "primarily," and "second."

Using precise language and domain-specific vocabulary

When writing informational or explanatory texts, it is vital to use precise language and domain-specific vocabulary to put forth your thesis and related ideas. Generalized vocabulary will do little to bring the points that you are making home to the audience, since they will not accurately reflect your thesis or supporting details. Domain-specific vocabulary is important to utilize because it will accurately describe or explain the ideas or processes that you are addressing. When you research a subject, make sure to familiarize yourself with any vocabulary that is involved in its explanation. Use dictionaries, if necessary, a technical dictionary, to decode any words you are not familiar with as well as context clues.

Establishing and maintaining a formal style

When writing an informational or explanatory text, it is important to establish and maintain a formal style of writing. Do not use a colloquial or casual tone. It is necessary to use the third person and to make the sentences longer and more complex. It is also important not to use any contractions when you write. A formal style announces that the writer is serious about his or her subject and wants to do it justice by keeping the thesis and supporting details clear, to the point, but as complex as they need to be. A formal style also means that the writer will not be interjecting a personal opinion that is not justified.

Importance of a concluding statement

A concluding statement or section that follows from and supports the information or explanation is important to a text, be it informational or explanatory because the conclusion helps to focus the important points in a text and also provides closure to the reader or audience. A good conclusion attempts to "wrap up" the passage so that the audience is made aware of a logical ending to the thesis. Without an effective conclusion, the passage would not have the weight it needs to have an impact. The conclusion should not make the reader feel that there is more information to follow, but rather set the tone for the ending of the argument by being reassuring and reiterating the important parts of the passage.

Narratives

Establishing a point of view

When writing a narrative, a story line or plot should be conceived that will allow for a narrator and characters as well as the point of view of the narrator as well as the author. The author's viewpoint will not necessarily be the same as the narrator's viewpoint. Points of view can be shown through dialogue or the way the narrator reacts to what characters do in the story. The characters will need to be drawn very clearly through both their descriptions; the author can hide his point of view in the characters' thoughts or actions. The narrator's point of view is usually more overtly seen in what is said in the narrative by the narrator.

Discuss the character and point of view in the following passage:

> The mouse ran though the hole. She saw the cheese. She grabbed it, but then she
> heard noises. She couldn't make it back to the hole. She was terrified. She ran under
> a chair and remained there until it was quiet. Then she ate the cheese.

The author has chosen to tell the narrative from the point of view of the mouse. This makes the mouse more human and more attractive to the reader. The author gives the mouse human characteristics; the mouse feels and can also reason. The author has created a character out of the mouse by concentrating on it and telling what it does. This is one way an author can establish the point of view of a character in a narrative. It is not clear what the point of view of the author is, but this could come later in the narrative.

Sequence of events

Sequence of events in a narrative should come naturally and logically out of the action and the plot. Rather than being forced, the sequence should follow the natural flow of a dialogue or plot and enhance what happens in the story. The only time that sequence is bypassed is when an author decides to use a literary device such as a flashback, which means the action does not flow in sequence but rather jumps back and forth. Events in a narrative are extremely important in helping the reader understand the intent or message of a narrative. When reading a narrative, take note of the order in which events occur to give a broader understanding of the passage.

Techniques used by the author

There are many techniques that authors employ to make their narratives come alive and have meaning. Among them, dialogue is an important factor, since it not only lets you know what is happening in a narrative, but it also colors what a character is like. The reader can tell from what a character says and how the character says it what the character feels about the events in a narrative. Equally important is the pacing that an author employs in revealing the nature of the characters and the kind of plot that is unraveling. This helps color the experiences and events in a narrative and increases the sensitivity of the audience. A third technique that broadens a narrative is the use of descriptions that help you visualize a character, what is happening, and what the character is doing.

Importance of transition words

Use of transition words are very important when writing a narrative. They can color the plot and the characters. They can also indicate the passage of time or the sequence of events. Sequence words, such as "first," "second," and "last," assist the reader in understanding the order in which events occur, which can be important to the flow of the plot. Words such as "then" and "next" also show the order in which events occur. "After a while" and "before this" are other sequence expressions. A change in setting can also be indicated. For instance, a passage may say, "First we went into the living room to talk," but later on it might say, "after we chatted for a while, we went into the dining room." This shows a shift in setting. When reading, notice transition words and their effect on the action.

Importance of language

How language is used is extremely important in a narrative. Precise language can help a reader gain an insight into character through a description. Details of what characters do and the setting or events in a narrative are also important and should be written in as lively and thought-provoking a manner as possible. Sensory language helps convey the mood and feeling of the setting and characters and will bring insight into the theme of a narrative. When reading, take special care to understand the range of language that an author employs in order to better comprehend the meaning of a narrative.

Role of a conclusion

The conclusion to a narrative is of the utmost importance, and without it a reader may end up feeling somewhat cheated by the experience of reading a story. The conclusion to a narrative is the resolution of the problem that is faced by the characters. The conclusion may not always be clear

- 172 -

cut; it may leave some questions unanswered. But the conclusion should give the reader the sense that the narrative is over, whatever the outcome. Traditionally, in tragedies the conclusion is one of sadness. On the other hand, in comedies the conclusion is light-hearted. In modern literature, conclusions can be much more evasive than they are in traditional literature, which leaves the reader often with more questions than answers.

Describe what he should look for when trying to come up with a good conclusion:

> Charles is writing a short story about a girl running for school president. He writes about all that she has done to win the election. Now he is looking for a conclusion to his story.

Charles should look for a conclusion that brings the story together. If the story is about a girl running for school president and what she has done to win the election, it probably should conclude with whether she won the election or not. There are other possibilities also, but this is the most obvious conclusion that the story should have. A conclusion should bring the entire story to a fitting and appropriate ending so that the reader has a sense of closure. It should follow the opening and the many events that happen, so that there is a form to the story.

Practice Test

Written Composition

Write a composition about a time when you made a hard decision.

Sample Composition

Last November, I was sitting in my third period math class when my teacher told me that she needed to talk to me after class. I was worried that I had done something wrong or had forgotten to turn in a homework assignment. I thought about it, but could not remember missing any assignments. I also thought that maybe I had failed the last test, but I felt that I had done well on it. When I finally talked to her, I was relieved to hear that she wanted to move me up into the accelerated math class. I immediately thought of my friend, Alex. He and I were in the same math class, and it was the only class we had together. I wanted to be in accelerated math, but I did not want to leave my friend.

When I came home from school, I told my parents what my teacher had said. "Wow!" my mom said, "That is great!" My dad smiled at me. "Good job," he said. "I am really proud of you." It made me happy to know that my parents were proud and excited for me. I was excited too, but I was also scared. I decided to talk to my mom about it. I told her that I did not want to leave class with Alex because we had no other classes together and that I was afraid. "What are you afraid of?" she asked. I told her that I was already behind in the accelerated math class, and that I was afraid I would not be able to catch up. I was also afraid that the class would be too hard for me.

"Well, that's a lot to think about," my mom said. She told me to look at everything I was afraid of and think about each thing. She said I needed a plan. She told me that if my teacher thought I could do well in the accelerated class, I should listen to her and believe in myself. I told her I thought that I could spend extra time with the new teacher learning the material that I had missed. "But what about Alex?" I said. I still did not want to leave my friend. "You always have recess," she said.

I decided to join the accelerated math class and am very happy. It was hard at first to keep up with the work that I had missed, but I like learning new things. I have made a lot of new friends, but I also see Alex at recess. We all have fun. The accelerated math class was better for me, and I am happy I made this hard decision.

Study Strategy

Being prepared for the test is necessary to combat anxiety, but what does being prepared look like? You may study for hours on end and still not feel prepared. What you need is a strategy for test prep. The next few pages outline our recommended steps to help you plan out and conquer the challenge of preparation.

Step 1: Scope Out the Test

Learn everything you can about the format (multiple choice, essay, etc.) and what will be on the test. Gather any study materials, course outlines, or sample exams that may be available. Not only will this help you to prepare, but knowing what to expect can help to alleviate test anxiety.

Step 2: Map Out the Material

Look through the textbook or study guide and make note of how many chapters or sections it has. Then divide these over the time you have. For example, if a book has 15 chapters and you have five days to study, you need to cover three chapters each day. Even better, if you have the time, leave an extra day at the end for overall review after you have gone through the material in depth.

If time is limited, you may need to prioritize the material. Look through it and make note of which sections you think you already have a good grasp on, and which need review. While you are studying, skim quickly through the familiar sections and take more time on the challenging parts. Write out your plan so you don't get lost as you go. Having a written plan also helps you feel more in control of the study, so anxiety is less likely to arise from feeling overwhelmed at the amount to cover. A sample plan may look like this:

- Day 1: Skim chapters 1–4, study chapter 5 (especially pages 31–33)
- Day 2: Study chapters 6–7, skim chapters 8–9
- Day 3: Skim chapter 10, study chapters 11–12 (especially pages 87–90)
- Day 4: Study chapters 13–15
- Day 5: Overall review (focus most on chapters 5, 6, and 12), take practice test

Step 3: Gather Your Tools

Decide what study method works best for you. Do you prefer to highlight in the book as you study and then go back over the highlighted portions? Or do you type out notes of the important information? Or is it helpful to make flashcards that you can carry with you? Assemble the pens, index cards, highlighters, post-it notes, and any other materials you may need so you won't be distracted by getting up to find things while you study.

If you're having a hard time retaining the information or organizing your notes, experiment with different methods. For example, try color-coding by subject with colored pens, highlighters, or post-it notes. If you learn better by hearing, try recording yourself reading your notes so you can listen while in the car, working out, or simply sitting at your desk. Ask a friend to quiz you from your flashcards, or try teaching someone the material to solidify it in your mind.

Step 4: Create Your Environment

It's important to avoid distractions while you study. This includes both the obvious distractions like visitors and the subtle distractions like an uncomfortable chair (or a too-comfortable couch that makes you want to fall asleep). Set up the best study environment possible: good lighting and a comfortable work area. If background music helps you focus, you may want to turn it on, but otherwise keep the room quiet. If you are using a computer to take notes, be sure you don't have any other windows open, especially applications like social media, games, or anything else that could distract you. Silence your phone and turn off notifications. Be sure to keep water close by so you stay hydrated while you study (but avoid unhealthy drinks and snacks).

Also, take into account the best time of day to study. Are you freshest first thing in the morning? Try to set aside some time then to work through the material. Is your mind clearer in the afternoon or evening? Schedule your study session then. Another method is to study at the same time of day that you will take the test, so that your brain gets used to working on the material at that time and will be ready to focus at test time.

Step 5: Study!

Once you have done all the study preparation, it's time to settle into the actual studying. Sit down, take a few moments to settle your mind so you can focus, and begin to follow your study plan. Don't give in to distractions or let yourself procrastinate. This is your time to prepare so you'll be ready to fearlessly approach the test. Make the most of the time and stay focused.

Of course, you don't want to burn out. If you study too long you may find that you're not retaining the information very well. Take regular study breaks. For example, taking five minutes out of every hour to walk briskly, breathing deeply and swinging your arms, can help your mind stay fresh.

As you get to the end of each chapter or section, it's a good idea to do a quick review. Remind yourself of what you learned and work on any difficult parts. When you feel that you've mastered the material, move on to the next part. At the end of your study session, briefly skim through your notes again.

But while review is helpful, cramming last minute is NOT. If at all possible, work ahead so that you won't need to fit all your study into the last day. Cramming overloads your brain with more information than it can process and retain, and your tired mind may struggle to recall even previously learned information when it is overwhelmed with last-minute study. Also, the urgent nature of cramming and the stress placed on your brain contribute to anxiety. You'll be more likely to go to the test feeling unprepared and having trouble thinking clearly.

So don't cram, and don't stay up late before the test, even just to review your notes at a leisurely pace. Your brain needs rest more than it needs to go over the information again. In fact, plan to finish your studies by noon or early afternoon the day before the test. Give your brain the rest of the day to relax or focus on other things, and get a good night's sleep. Then you will be fresh for the test and better able to recall what you've studied.

Step 6: Take a practice test

Many courses offer sample tests, either online or in the study materials. This is an excellent resource to check whether you have mastered the material, as well as to prepare for the test format and environment.

Check the test format ahead of time: the number of questions, the type (multiple choice, free response, etc.), and the time limit. Then create a plan for working through them. For example, if you have 30 minutes to take a 60-question test, your limit is 30 seconds per question. Spend less time on the questions you know well so that you can take more time on the difficult ones.

If you have time to take several practice tests, take the first one open book, with no time limit. Work through the questions at your own pace and make sure you fully understand them. Gradually work up to taking a test under test conditions: sit at a desk with all study materials put away and set a timer. Pace yourself to make sure you finish the test with time to spare and go back to check your answers if you have time.

After each test, check your answers. On the questions you missed, be sure you understand why you missed them. Did you misread the question (tests can use tricky wording)? Did you forget the information? Or was it something you hadn't learned? Go back and study any shaky areas that the practice tests reveal.

Taking these tests not only helps with your grade, but also aids in combating test anxiety. If you're already used to the test conditions, you're less likely to worry about it, and working through tests until you're scoring well gives you a confidence boost. Go through the practice tests until you feel comfortable, and then you can go into the test knowing that you're ready for it.

Test Tips

On test day, you should be confident, knowing that you've prepared well and are ready to answer the questions. But aside from preparation, there are several test day strategies you can employ to maximize your performance.

First, as stated before, get a good night's sleep the night before the test (and for several nights before that, if possible). Go into the test with a fresh, alert mind rather than staying up late to study.

Try not to change too much about your normal routine on the day of the test. It's important to eat a nutritious breakfast, but if you normally don't eat breakfast at all, consider eating just a protein bar. If you're a coffee drinker, go ahead and have your normal coffee. Just make sure you time it so that the caffeine doesn't wear off right in the middle of your test. Avoid sugary beverages, and drink enough water to stay hydrated but not so much that you need a restroom break 10 minutes into the test. If your test isn't first thing in the morning, consider going for a walk or doing a light workout before the test to get your blood flowing.

Allow yourself enough time to get ready, and leave for the test with plenty of time to spare so you won't have the anxiety of scrambling to arrive in time. Another reason to be early is to select a good seat. It's helpful to sit away from doors and windows, which can be distracting. Find a good seat, get out your supplies, and settle your mind before the test begins.

When the test begins, start by going over the instructions carefully, even if you already know what to expect. Make sure you avoid any careless mistakes by following the directions.

Then begin working through the questions, pacing yourself as you've practiced. If you're not sure on an answer, don't spend too much time on it, and don't let it shake your confidence. Either skip it and come back later, or eliminate as many wrong answers as possible and guess among the remaining ones. Don't dwell on these questions as you continue—put them out of your mind and focus on what lies ahead.

Be sure to read all of the answer choices, even if you're sure the first one is the right answer. Sometimes you'll find a better one if you keep reading. But don't second-guess yourself if you do immediately know the answer. Your gut instinct is usually right. Don't let test anxiety rob you of the information you know.

If you have time at the end of the test (and if the test format allows), go back and review your answers. Be cautious about changing any, since your first instinct tends to be correct, but make sure you didn't misread any of the questions or accidentally mark the wrong answer choice. Look over any you skipped and make an educated guess.

At the end, leave the test feeling confident. You've done your best, so don't waste time worrying about your performance or wishing you could change anything. Instead, celebrate the successful completion of this test. And finally, use this test to learn how to deal with anxiety even better next time.

> **Review Video: 5 Tips to Beat Test Anxiety**
> Visit mometrix.com/academy and enter code: 570656

Important Qualification

Not all anxiety is created equal. If your test anxiety is causing major issues in your life beyond the classroom or testing center, or if you are experiencing troubling physical symptoms related to your anxiety, it may be a sign of a serious physiological or psychological condition. If this sounds like your situation, we strongly encourage you to seek professional help.

How to Overcome Your Fear of Math

The word *math* is enough to strike fear into most hearts. How many of us have memories of sitting through confusing lectures, wrestling over mind-numbing homework, or taking tests that still seem incomprehensible even after hours of study? Years after graduation, many still shudder at these memories.

The fact is, math is not just a classroom subject. It has real-world implications that you face every day, whether you realize it or not. This may be balancing your monthly budget, deciding how many supplies to buy for a project, or simply splitting a meal check with friends. The idea of daily confrontations with math can be so paralyzing that some develop a condition known as *math anxiety*.

But you do NOT need to be paralyzed by this anxiety! In fact, while you may have thought all your life that you're not good at math, or that your brain isn't wired to understand it, the truth is that you may have been conditioned to think this way. From your earliest school days, the way you were taught affected the way you viewed different subjects. And the way math has been taught has changed.

Several decades ago, there was a shift in American math classrooms. The focus changed from traditional problem-solving to a conceptual view of topics, de-emphasizing the importance of learning the basics and building on them. The solid foundation necessary for math progression and confidence was undermined. Math became more of a vague concept than a concrete idea. Today, it is common to think of math, not as a straightforward system, but as a mysterious, complicated method that can't be fully understood unless you're a genius.

This is why you may still have nightmares about being called on to answer a difficult problem in front of the class. Math anxiety is a very real, though unnecessary, fear.

Math anxiety may begin with a single class period. Let's say you missed a day in 6th grade math and never quite understood the concept that was taught while you were gone. Since math is cumulative, with each new concept building on past ones, this could very well affect the rest of your math career. Without that one day's knowledge, it will be difficult to understand any other concepts that link to it. Rather than realizing that you're just missing one key piece, you may begin to believe that you're simply not capable of understanding math.

This belief can change the way you approach other classes, career options, and everyday life experiences, if you become anxious at the thought that math might be required. A student who loves science may choose a different path of study upon realizing that multiple math classes will be required for a degree. An aspiring medical student may hesitate at the thought of going through the necessary math classes. For some this anxiety escalates into a more extreme state known as *math phobia*.

Math anxiety is challenging to address because it is rooted deeply and may come from a variety of causes: an embarrassing moment in class, a teacher who did not explain concepts well and contributed to a shaky foundation, or a failed test that contributed to the belief of math failure.

These causes add up over time, encouraged by society's popular view that math is hard and unpleasant. Eventually a person comes to firmly believe that he or she is simply bad at math. This belief makes it difficult to grasp new concepts or even remember old ones. Homework and test grades begin to slip, which only confirms the belief. The poor performance is not due to lack of ability but is caused by math anxiety.

Math anxiety is an emotional issue, not a lack of intelligence. But when it becomes deeply rooted, it can become more than just an emotional problem. Physical symptoms appear. Blood pressure may rise and heartbeat may quicken at the sight of a math problem – or even the thought of math! This fear leads to a mental block. When someone with math anxiety is asked to perform a calculation, even a basic problem can seem overwhelming and impossible. The emotional and physical response to the thought of math prevents the brain from working through it logically.

The more this happens, the more a person's confidence drops, and the more math anxiety is generated. This vicious cycle must be broken!

The first step in breaking the cycle is to go back to very beginning and make sure you really understand the basics of how math works and why it works. It is not enough to memorize rules for multiplication and division. If you don't know WHY these rules work, your foundation will be shaky and you will be at risk of developing a phobia. Understanding mathematical concepts not only promotes confidence and security, but allows you to build on this understanding for new concepts. Additionally, you can solve unfamiliar problems using familiar concepts and processes.

Why is it that students in other countries regularly outperform American students in math? The answer likely boils down to a couple of things: the foundation of mathematical conceptual understanding and societal perception. While students in the US are not expected to *like* or *get* math, in many other nations, students are expected not only to understand math but also to excel at it.

Changing the American view of math that leads to math anxiety is a monumental task. It requires changing the training of teachers nationwide, from kindergarten through high school, so that they learn to teach the *why* behind math and to combat the wrong math views that students may develop. It also involves changing the stigma associated with math, so that it is no longer viewed as unpleasant and incomprehensible. While these are necessary changes, they are challenging and will take time. But in the meantime, math anxiety is not irreversible—it can be faced and defeated, one person at a time.

False Beliefs

One reason math anxiety has taken such hold is that several false beliefs have been created and shared until they became widely accepted. Some of these unhelpful beliefs include the following:

There is only one way to solve a math problem. In the same way that you can choose from different driving routes and still arrive at the same house, you can solve a math problem using different methods and still find the correct answer. A person who understands the reasoning behind math calculations may be able to look at an unfamiliar concept and find the right answer, just by applying logic to the knowledge they already have. This approach may be different than what is taught in the classroom, but it is still valid. Unfortunately, even many teachers view math as a subject where the best course of action is to memorize the rule or process for each problem rather than as a place for students to exercise logic and creativity in finding a solution.

Many people don't have a mind for math. A person who has struggled due to poor teaching or math anxiety may falsely believe that he or she doesn't have the mental capacity to grasp mathematical concepts. Most of the time, this is false. Many people find that when they are relieved of their math anxiety, they have more than enough brainpower to understand math.

Men are naturally better at math than women. Even though research has shown this to be false, many young women still avoid math careers and classes because of their belief that their math abilities are inferior. Many girls have come to believe that math is a male skill and have given up trying to understand or enjoy it.

Counting aids are bad. Something like counting on your fingers or drawing out a problem to visualize it may be frowned on as childish or a crutch, but these devices can help you get a tangible understanding of a problem or a concept.

Sadly, many students buy into these ideologies at an early age. A young girl who enjoys math class may be conditioned to think that she doesn't actually have the brain for it because math is for boys, and may turn her energies to other pursuits, permanently closing the door on a wide range of opportunities. A child who finds the right answer but doesn't follow the teacher's method may believe that he is doing it wrong and isn't good at math. A student who never had a problem with math before may have a poor teacher and become confused, yet believe that the problem is because she doesn't have a mathematical mind.

Students who have bought into these erroneous beliefs quickly begin to add their own anxieties, adapting them to their own personal situations:

I'll never use this in real life. A huge number of people wrongly believe that math is irrelevant outside the classroom. By adopting this mindset, they are handicapping themselves for a life in a mathematical world, as well as limiting their career choices. When they are inevitably faced with real-world math, they are conditioning themselves to respond with anxiety.

I'm not quick enough. While timed tests and quizzes, or even simply comparing yourself with other students in the class, can lead to this belief, speed is not an indicator of skill level. A person can work very slowly yet understand at a deep level.

If I can understand it, it's too easy. People with a low view of their own abilities tend to think that if they are able to grasp a concept, it must be simple. They cannot accept the idea that they are capable of understanding math. This belief will make it harder to learn, no matter how intelligent they are.

I just can't learn this. An overwhelming number of people think this, from young children to adults, and much of the time it is simply not true. But this mindset can turn into a self-fulfilling prophecy that keeps you from exercising and growing your math ability.

The good news is, each of these myths can be debunked. For most people, they are based on emotion and psychology, NOT on actual ability! It will take time, effort, and the desire to change, but change is possible. Even if you have spent years thinking that you don't have the capability to understand math, it is not too late to uncover your true ability and find relief from the anxiety that surrounds math.

Math Strategies

It is important to have a plan of attack to combat math anxiety. There are many useful strategies for pinpointing the fears or myths and eradicating them:

Go back to the basics. For most people, math anxiety stems from a poor foundation. You may think that you have a complete understanding of addition and subtraction, or even decimals and percentages, but make absolutely sure. Learning math is different from learning other subjects. For example, when you learn history, you study various time periods and places and events. It may be important to memorize dates or find out about the lives of famous people. When you move from US history to world history, there will be some overlap, but a large amount of the information will be new. Mathematical concepts, on the other hand, are very closely linked and highly dependent on each other. It's like climbing a ladder – if a rung is missing from your understanding, it may be difficult or impossible for you to climb any higher, no matter how hard you try. So go back and make sure your math foundation is strong. This may mean taking a remedial math course, going to a tutor to work through the shaky concepts, or just going through your old homework to make sure you really understand it.

Speak the language. Math has a large vocabulary of terms and phrases unique to working problems. Sometimes these are completely new terms, and sometimes they are common words, but are used differently in a math setting. If you can't speak the language, it will be very difficult to get a thorough understanding of the concepts. It's common for students to think that they don't understand math when they simply don't understand the vocabulary. The good news is that this is fairly easy to fix. Brushing up on any terms you aren't quite sure of can help bring the rest of the concepts into focus.

Check your anxiety level. When you think about math, do you feel nervous or uncomfortable? Do you struggle with feelings of inadequacy, even on concepts that you know you've already learned? It's important to understand your specific math anxieties, and what triggers them. When you catch yourself falling back on a false belief, mentally replace it with the truth. Don't let yourself believe that you can't learn, or that struggling with a concept means you'll never understand it. Instead, remind yourself of how much you've already learned and dwell on that past success. Visualize grasping the new concept, linking it to your old knowledge, and moving on to the next challenge. Also, learn how to manage anxiety when it arises. There are many techniques for coping with the irrational fears that rise to the surface when you enter the math classroom. This may include controlled breathing, replacing negative thoughts with positive ones, or visualizing success. Anxiety interferes with your ability to concentrate and absorb information, which in turn contributes to greater anxiety. If you can learn how to regain control of your thinking, you will be better able to pay attention, make progress, and succeed!

Don't go it alone. Like any deeply ingrained belief, math anxiety is not easy to eradicate. And there is no need for you to wrestle through it on your own. It will take time, and many people find that speaking with a counselor or psychiatrist helps. They can help you develop strategies for responding to anxiety and overcoming old ideas. Additionally, it can be very helpful to take a short course or seek out a math tutor to help you find and fix the missing rungs on your ladder and make sure that you're ready to progress to the next level. You can also find a number of math aids online: courses that will teach you mental devices for figuring out problems, how to get the most out of your math classes, etc.

Check your math attitude. No matter how much you want to learn and overcome your anxiety, you'll have trouble if you still have a negative attitude toward math. If you think it's too hard, or just have general feelings of dread about math, it will be hard to learn and to break through the anxiety. Work on cultivating a positive math attitude. Remind yourself that math is not just a hurdle to be cleared, but a valuable asset. When you view math with a positive attitude, you'll be much more likely to understand and even enjoy it. This is something you must do for yourself. You may find it helpful to visit with a counselor. Your tutor, friends, and family may cheer you on in your endeavors. But your greatest asset is yourself. You are inside your own mind – tell yourself what you need to hear. Relive past victories. Remind yourself that you are capable of understanding math. Root out any false beliefs that linger and replace them with positive truths. Even if it doesn't feel true at first, it will begin to affect your thinking and pave the way for a positive, anxiety-free mindset.

Aside from these general strategies, there are a number of specific practical things you can do to begin your journey toward overcoming math anxiety. Something as simple as learning a new note-taking strategy can change the way you approach math and give you more confidence and understanding. New study techniques can also make a huge difference.

Math anxiety leads to bad habits. If it causes you to be afraid of answering a question in class, you may gravitate toward the back row. You may be embarrassed to ask for help. And you may procrastinate on assignments, which leads to rushing through them at the last moment when it's too late to get a better understanding. It's important to identify your negative behaviors and replace them with positive ones:

Prepare ahead of time. Read the lesson before you go to class. Being exposed to the topics that will be covered in class ahead of time, even if you don't understand them perfectly, is extremely helpful in increasing what you retain from the lecture. Do your homework and, if you're still shaky, go over some extra problems. The key to a solid understanding of math is practice.

Sit front and center. When you can easily see and hear, you'll understand more, and you'll avoid the distractions of other students if no one is in front of you. Plus, you're more likely to be sitting with students who are positive and engaged, rather than others with math anxiety. Let their positive math attitude rub off on you.

Ask questions in class and out. If you don't understand something, just ask. If you need a more in-depth explanation, the teacher may need to work with you outside of class, but often it's a simple concept you don't quite understand, and a single question may clear it up. If you wait, you may not be able to follow the rest of the day's lesson. For extra help, most professors have office hours outside of class when you can go over concepts one-on-one to clear up any uncertainties. Additionally, there may be a *math lab* or study session you can attend for homework help. Take advantage of this.

Review. Even if you feel that you've fully mastered a concept, review it periodically to reinforce it. Going over an old lesson has several benefits: solidifying your understanding, giving you a confidence boost, and even giving some new insights into material that you're currently learning! Don't let yourself get rusty. That can lead to problems with learning later concepts.

Teaching Tips

While the math student's mindset is the most crucial to overcoming math anxiety, it is also important for others to adjust their math attitudes. Teachers and parents have an enormous influence on how students relate to math. They can either contribute to math confidence or math anxiety.

As a parent or teacher, it is very important to convey a positive math attitude. Retelling horror stories of your own bad experience with math will contribute to a new generation of math anxiety. Even if you don't share your experiences, others will be able to sense your fears and may begin to believe them.

Even a careless comment can have a big impact, so watch for phrases like *He's not good at math* or *I never liked math*. You are a crucial role model, and your children or students will unconsciously adopt your mindset. Give them a positive example to follow. Rather than teaching them to fear the math world before they even know it, teach them about all its potential and excitement.

Work to present math as an integral, beautiful, and understandable part of life. Encourage creativity in solving problems. Watch for false beliefs and dispel them. Cross the lines between subjects: integrate history, English, and music with math. Show students how math is used every day, and how the entire world is based on mathematical principles, from the pull of gravity to the shape of seashells. Instead of letting students see math as a necessary evil, direct them to view it as an imaginative, beautiful art form – an art form that they are capable of mastering and using.

Don't give too narrow a view of math. It is more than just numbers. Yes, working problems and learning formulas is a large part of classroom math. But don't let the teaching stop there. Teach students about the everyday implications of math. Show them how nature works according to the laws of mathematics, and take them outside to make discoveries of their own. Expose them to math-related careers by inviting visiting speakers, asking students to do research and presentations, and learning students' interests and aptitudes on a personal level.

Demonstrate the importance of math. Many people see math as nothing more than a required stepping stone to their degree, a nuisance with no real usefulness. Teach students that algebra is used every day in managing their bank accounts, in following recipes, and in scheduling the day's events. Show them how learning to do geometric proofs helps them to develop logical thinking, an invaluable life skill. Let them see that math surrounds them and is integrally linked to their daily lives: that weather predictions are based on math, that math was used to design cars and other machines, etc. Most of all, give them the tools to use math to enrich their lives.

Make math as tangible as possible. Use visual aids and objects that can be touched. It is much easier to grasp a concept when you can hold it in your hands and manipulate it, rather than just listening to the lecture. Encourage math outside of the classroom. The real world is full of measuring, counting, and calculating, so let students participate in this. Keep your eyes open for numbers and patterns to discuss. Talk about how scores are calculated in sports games and how far apart plants are placed in a garden row for maximum growth. Build the mindset that math is a normal and interesting part of daily life.

Finally, find math resources that help to build a positive math attitude. There are a number of books that show math as fascinating and exciting while teaching important concepts, for example: *The Math Curse; A Wrinkle in Time; The Phantom Tollbooth;* and *Fractals, Googols and Other Mathematical Tales.* You can also find a number of online resources: math puzzles and games, videos that show math in nature, and communities of math enthusiasts. On a local level, students can compete in a variety of math competitions with other schools or join a math club.

The student who experiences math as exciting and interesting is unlikely to suffer from math anxiety. Going through life without this handicap is an immense advantage and opens many doors that others have closed through their fear.

Self-Check

Whether you suffer from math anxiety or not, chances are that you have been exposed to some of the false beliefs mentioned above. Now is the time to check yourself for any errors you may have accepted. Do you think you're not wired for math? Or that you don't need to understand it since you're not planning on a math career? Do you think math is just too difficult for the average person?

Find the errors you've taken to heart and replace them with positive thinking. Are you capable of learning math? Yes! Can you control your anxiety? Yes! These errors will resurface from time to time, so be watchful. Don't let others with math anxiety influence you or sway your confidence. If you're having trouble with a concept, find help. Don't let it discourage you!

Create a plan of attack for defeating math anxiety and sharpening your skills. Do some research and decide if it would help you to take a class, get a tutor, or find some online resources to fine-tune your knowledge. Make the effort to get good nutrition, hydration, and sleep so that you are operating at full capacity. Remind yourself daily that you are skilled and that anxiety does not control you. Your mind is capable of so much more than you know. Give it the tools it needs to grow and thrive.

Thank You

We at Mometrix would like to extend our heartfelt thanks to you, our friend and patron, for allowing us to play a part in your journey. It is a privilege to serve people from all walks of life who are unified in their commitment to building the best future they can for themselves.

The preparation you devote to these important testing milestones may be the most valuable educational opportunity you have for making a real difference in your life. We encourage you to put your heart into it—that feeling of succeeding, overcoming, and yes, conquering will be well worth the hours you've invested.

We want to hear your story, your struggles and your successes, and if you see any opportunities for us to improve our materials so we can help others even more effectively in the future, please share that with us as well. **The team at Mometrix would be absolutely thrilled to hear from you!** So please, send us an email (support@mometrix.com) and let's stay in touch.

If you'd like some additional help, check out these other resources we offer for your exam:

http://MometrixFlashcards.com/ACTAspire

Additional Bonus Material

Due to our efforts to try to keep this book to a manageable length, we've created a link that will give you access to all of your additional bonus material.

Please visit https://www.mometrix.com/bonus948/actaspireg7 to access the information.